Meanderings

MEG MANLY

ISBN: 1973883287
ISBN-13: 978-1973883289

DEDICATION

To my much-loved children: John, Margaret, Sarah,
Jo and Tom.

ABOUT THE AUTHOR

Margaret ("Meg") Manly was born in Chesterfield, Derbyshire. Her family moved to South Wales when she was 12 and then, following the outbreak of World War II, to Chester. Meg now lives in Suffolk. She has always enjoyed "scribbling" as well as painting; in her '90s, she decided to write her first book: memories of life in the '20s, '30s and beyond. She invites her readers to "meander" down memory lane with her.

ACKNOWLEDGMENTS

My heartfelt thanks to my daughter, Margaret, and good friend, Louise, for preparing and publishing this book and for encouraging me to believe that I could write it.

MEANDERINGS

INTRODUCTION

By 1906 my maternal grandfather, John Henry Whitworth, had saved his first thousand pounds and used it to have a pair of houses built: numbers 16 and 18 Tennyson Avenue in the Derbyshire market town of Chesterfield. He and his wife Annie and their eight-year-old daughter, Evelyn, together with his mother-in-law lived in no. 16 and no. 18 was rented out.

When Evelyn grew up she married Maynard Cecil Cook who lived in nearby Queen Street and whom she had known for most of her life. They then took over the tenancy of no. 18 and in 1922 had a baby boy, christening him John Maynard. Two years later they produced me.

I cannot claim to have any memories of my birth but I have been reliably informed that it took place rather abruptly at the inconvenient hour of 2am on 19th August 1924. I was christened Margaret Dorothy. Years later I told Mother that I had always disliked the name Dorothy and asked her why she had chosen it. Her answer has always baffled me. "Oh," she said, "it was because it was the doctor's favourite name."

Not long before she died, my mother told me that she wished that she had asked her Granny and her parents about their early lives. I, too, in my turn have regretted not asking my parents what life was like when they were young. So I am now writing this account of my memories, interspersed with some of theirs, firstly until the outbreak of the Second World War, and, secondly, from then until peace was declared in 1945 when I was 21 years old, married and had left my parents' home.

CHAPTER ONE

When my brother and I were very young, we were well looked after by Robbie, who was what was called a "Mother's Help". She loved us and we loved her, which was as well because there were times when Mother would be away from home. Mother had been a rather cossetted only child and was thought of as delicate. Consequently she would take herself off to her beloved Bournemouth for the sake of her health and to meet up with the friends she had there. Sometimes she would take John with her as he, too, was considered to benefit from those visits. I was told in later years that they had both had pneumonia and been "at death's door", which would account for a lot.

I was always considered to be fit and healthy, despite having been born with a twisted bowel. This must have entailed time spent in a hospital because if ever I didn't want to eat what was put on my plate, I was told: "Finish it or Sister will be cross". That was better than the stupid and unfair threat that some mothers used – "or we'll have to tell your father when he comes home". The idea of making the other parent into a source of fear and retribution always struck me as being stupid as well as being grossly unfair.

It was those visits to Bournemouth that gave rise to my two earliest and very distinct memories of not recognising my mother, neither of which I ever mentioned to her. Initially, I suppose because it didn't matter to me and later because there would have been no reason to do so and it would have been hurtful to her to bring up something that she herself had probably forgotten.

On the first occasion I would have been about 18 months old and I was sitting on the floor when the door opened and a lady came in. She was wearing a grey dress. I don't suppose I knew the word "grey" at the time but when I did know the names of colours I recognised it as the colour that the lady had been wearing. She began to cry and my father, who was standing a little behind and to the side of her, gave her his handkerchief. Of what happened next I have no recollection; it seems likely that she was crying because she was my mother and I didn't know her.

Mother must have been away from home again on the second occasion when – a little older now – I remember sitting on Robbie's knee and then clambering all over her and suddenly pointing to a picture and asking, "Who is that?" "That's your Mummy," said Robbie. I don't remember having any reaction to this information; I think it had only been mild curiosity on my part. I have no memories of Mother either leaving or returning home at any time so I suppose I never experienced the sadness of saying goodbye to her or any joy at seeing her again when she came home.

"Robbie" was what we called Nurse Robinson; she was "Robbie" to everybody and never called anything else. She was about the same size as Mother but with dark hair as opposed to Mother's rather distinctive and lovely shade of blonde. Mother nearly didn't employ her because she had a stiff leg which caused her to limp. However, it didn't seem to slow her down and she could climb the stairs as quickly as Mother could.

She came from a village called Hathersage and one day she took me on a visit there. The only part I can remember is meeting her brother who owned a motorbike. I was thrilled with this machine, especially as he let me sit on the pillion whilst he slowly drove it a little way. I must have very stupidly told Mother of this wonderful ride because she told me years later how cross she had been as she thought that it was a dangerous thing to do. As if our beloved Robbie would have taken any risks with our safety!

The occasional absences of my mother were in no way upsetting to me and I never felt unloved or neglected in any way. I don't think that I was unusual in that whatever happened in my life as a child seemed a normal state of affairs. Although I never gave any thought to the matter, I loved my brother, my parents and my maternal grandparents and they loved me and never gave me any reason to doubt it.

On my forehead I still have a faint scar from a gash caused by my falling down two steps. My brother had previously tumbled down the whole flight of stairs; he had curled himself into a ball and wasn't harmed in any way. Apparently, I wasn't yet old enough to negotiate the stairs but was determined to try. All that I remember is pain, bawling my head off and Granny holding me in her arms. It must have been tea-time because my attention was caught by some little chocolate Swiss rolls; I can see them now. It was suggested that I might have one if I stopped crying – gluttony won!

I was a little older in my next memory but still quite small as I couldn't see beyond Grandma Cook's knees without tipping my head back. This is my only memory of my father's mother and it is not a good one. She must have spoken to me because I remember looking up at her and thinking, "I don't like you" and, almost immediately, "and you don't like me". This in no way bothered me, it was just something I accepted as a fact. I turned my gaze away from her to a low cupboard in what was probably a sideboard – I remember that it was dark and had short, twisted legs. I knew there were sometimes sweets or chocolates in there and I wondered if she would give me one. I don't remember whether or not she did but it shows yet again my abiding interest in chocolate.

Years later, I learned that I was right about our mutual dislike. Apparently, even in my pram I would not acknowledge her if we met in the street. I probably sensed her antipathy even then – children are like animals in that respect. On one occasion she complained angrily to my father that I wouldn't say "Good morning" to her although she knew that I was now able to talk. "You should make her say good morning, Maynard," she told him, whereupon my father, who shared my opinion of his mother, replied with some degree of satisfaction, "You try making my daughter do something she doesn't want to do." This would not have helped our relationship or theirs.

I don't think my father and his mother were ever close and maybe it's understandable. Father was the sole survivor of her five children, three of whom had died at birth. The fourth child, who was reputedly golden-haired and angelic, succumbed to diphtheria when he was two years old. It was said at the time that he was beautiful and "too good for this world". This would have been an impossible act for Father to follow; he had black hair and was probably not the least bit angelic. Life must have been dreadful for women in those days; so many children dying either at birth or at a very young age must have been heartbreaking. Grandma might have been a very different type of woman had she not experienced the loss of four of her children. On the other hand I heard that she was far more interested in going on frequent and rather expensive holidays than being at home with children, so who can tell.

Father never said much about his parents but he did tell me that his mother's maiden name was Alice Maria Harrison and both she and his father were from Lincolnshire. Alice Maria had three sisters, two of whom, Lucy and Sophia, couldn't have been more different from each other. One, he said, was a complete madcap and was supposedly one of the first women to go up in an air balloon. At some point she emigrated to Canada, but I don't know which of the sisters it was. I do remember when I was very small my father bringing his cousin Harold to see me before I went to sleep. I had been told that he was coming to see Daddy and that he was from a town called Toronto in Canada which was across the sea and a long way away. I remember all this because I found it so exciting.

The other sister, Father said, was a "religious maniac". Grandpa and Grandma must also have been of a religious turn of mind because years later I was shown the large family Bible in the front of which were recorded the births and deaths of their children. Father told me that they held family prayers every morning which their two maids also had to attend.

As soon as he was old enough Father was sent away to Worksop College as a boarder. This must have been an extremely religious-minded school as the pupils had to attend chapel four times on Sundays in addition to any other religious instruction which they may have received. This, together with the unpalatable school meals, resulted in my father making a solemn vow that when he left school he would never again eat rice pudding, nor would he enter a church except for weddings and funerals. To the best of my knowledge he kept his word.

Grandpa Cook owned a Ladies and Gentlemen's Outfitters on the High Street in Chesterfield. There were two entrances to this establishment but I only went into the one which led to the Ladies Clothing Department. I know they also sold Elizabeth Arden's range of cosmetics which Mother continued to use throughout her life. Upstairs there was what was probably a stock room and another room where any required alterations were carried out. In those days if a garment you chose wasn't already a perfect fit a fitter would come down from upstairs and put in the appropriate pins to mark where adjustments needed to be made. There were two alteration hands in the room above the shop and once I was taken to meet them. Alterations and fittings were all part of the service when I was a child and involved the customer in no extra cost.

Although I never really knew him, I understood that Grandpa Cook was a nice, gentle man. I thought of him as being tall but that may only have been in comparison with Grandma who was very short and dumpy. I also knew that he came from Lincolnshire but had no idea where that was. I did know a song about a Lincolnshire poacher. It starts something like this: "t'was my delight on a Friday night in the season of the year"; I have no idea what comes next, maybe I'll check it out one day. The point is that I was proudly convinced that my Grandpa was the

Lincolnshire Poacher. It was a great disappointment when I found that this claim to fame was groundless.

Secretly, though, at the back of my mind I clung on to my original idea. When I later heard that he was often asked for his expert opinion on whether or not a fur was genuine, I thought , "There you are then, he probably learned all that when he was a poacher". Grandpa would probably have been amused by this but I can imagine the outrage such a suggestion would have been to Grandma Cook. I think she may have had delusions of grandeur because my Great Granny sometimes referred to her as "The Duchess", as in "The Duchess is coming to tea today".

CHAPTER TWO

When Mother and John were away in Bournemouth I often stayed with my Granny and Grandad Whitworth who were much younger than my father's parents. Grandma and Grandpa Cook. I remember my bedroom very clearly. The bedspread on the big double bed was silky and old gold in colour. On the dressing table in the bay window was a lovely hand mirror, brush and comb, two glass scent bottles and a powder puff bowl, all decorated with blue enamel and silver gilt. There were two little Lalique pin trays as well. In front of the dressing table was a rug with a deep, soft pile that came up to my ankles.

On the bedside table were books but the only one that I remember being interested in was "The Rubaiyat of Omar Khayyam". I loved it long before I could understand it; the illustrations and the flow and sound of the words fascinated me. They still do because when my grandparents died the book was given to me. I inherited the dressing table set too, and the rug.

Indeed I remember the whole house very clearly and in greater detail than any other house I lived in as a child. I even remember the saucepans and lids hanging on the walls of the pantry; they shone so that you could see your face in them. These would have been polished by Elsie, the maid, who was a great one for polishing. She and I were good friends. She could play the accordion and taught me songs; the only one I can now recall contained the lines, "There ain't no sense sitting on the fence all by yourself in the moonlight", my rendering of which was not approved of by Granny.

The kitchen had a big well-scrubbed table in the middle, a Welsh dresser and a small table on top of which was a very old family Jones sewing machine which later became mine. There was a kitchen range, a gas stove, a deep sink with a wooden plate rack over it, an armchair and on the floor a big rag rug.

Family washing was done in the outside washhouse, part of a building which included a coal store, lavatory and a place for the garden tools and dustbins. In the washhouse was a large metal container called a copper in which you heated water to boil anything that needed sterilising or to remove stains. There were also a sink and a thing called a dolly for bashing things about in the copper and a big wooden mangle. I think that the sheets must have been sent to the laundry because I don't remember seeing them hanging on the clothes-line. What I do remember is that rugs were hung over the line and beaten with a carpet beater which looked somewhat like a rattan tennis racquet.

The garden, although quite small, had a lawn with a summerhouse at the far end and a wide flower border separating it from the garden of no. 18 next door. Grandad, who was no gardener, had this border planted each year as the seasons progressed with the same flowers: King Alfred daffodils followed by tulips, followed by geraniums. I think asters or dahlias followed on. Great Granny appropriated the border on the left-hand side between the outbuildings and the summerhouse, in which she grew Lilies of the Valley under the trees by the dividing wall.

It was not a garden to play games in, apart from the yard outside the back door where the wall was very high and you could play "knock-a-back" against it. If you don't know what "knock-a-back" is, and it may well be called by different names in other parts of the country, it involves throwing a ball at the wall and knocking it back with your hand, sometimes letting it bounce first. This procedure is varied by what you decide must be done between the ball rebounding and you knocking it back again, maybe hand-claps or turning around or whatever else you dreamed up. I suppose it was good training for coordination of hand and eye when playing other games and I daresay it is still played today wherever there is a suitable wall.

My first knowledge of death came when I was staying with my grandparents. I was about three years old when Granny came into my bedroom one morning and told me that Great Granny, of whom I now have only a faint memory, had died. Granny told me that the angels had come during the night with their horses and chariot and carried Great Granny away to live with God in Heaven. I had a mental picture of this and thought how nice that was and I was happy for her.

Great Granny had an interesting background. She ran away from home at the age of nineteen to marry James Cholerton, the son of a gardener employed at a country estate in Beeston. Her family considered this to be an unsuitable match for her; the general opinion was that she would be "marrying beneath her". Her brother must have approved of him as he elected to give the bride away at the wedding, her father having died some years before.

Elizabeth and James eventually went to live in Chesterfield, where he acquired a coach and plied for hire; a horse-drawn taxi, I suppose. They had four children but my Granny, Annie, was the only one who survived childhood. Her sister, Ethel was stillborn and her two brothers, George and Benjamin, succumbed to diphtheria in their teens. James must have made a success of his business as I know that my Granny learnt to play the violin and attended the Girls' High School until she was eighteen.

Great Granny was widowed at the age of 45 and lived with my Granny and Grandad, happily taking on the task of rearing my mother and generally running the household. This arrangement suited everybody as Granny was not at all interested in such matters; her ambition had always been to own a shop and she had begged her father to allow her to go out to work and get some experience. He refused to permit her to do this and she had to content herself with continuing to be a pupil teacher.

When James died at an early age, Granny got her wish and eventually took over the management of what was called a baby linen shop. Later when she met and married my grandfather, she worked with him, mainly in the florist side of his greengrocery business. She never became or needed to become domesticated. We used to say that she would be hard put to it to boil an egg. Great Granny had also been unable to cook when she married but was soon taught by her kind and friendly neighbour and very quickly proved to be an excellent cook, seamstress and household manager.

Great Granny's maiden name was Elizabeth Ann Evans and she was born and brought up in the village of Ellastone in Staffordshire. Her father, George, was a joiner, farmer and publican and he and his family lived at The Granville Arms, later known as The Duncombe Arms, an inn that after being closed for some years fairly recently reopened. Another inn, the Bromley Arms, was next door and it was there that George's wife, Ann Salt was born and lived until her marriage. My mother was often taken to stay in Ellastone by her grandmother and knew the descendants of both families.

The author George Eliot, whose real name was Mary Ann Evans, was my Great Granny's cousin. They shared the same grandfather, Thomas, but not the same grandmother, Thomas having married three times. Mary Ann's father, Robert, was for a time the village carpenter in Ellastone. The family originally came from Wales and settled in Norbury, a village just over the Staffordshire border into Derbyshire.

Great Granny owned copies of all of George Eliot's books. Granny was not interested in reading but my mother was and she read all of them. The only one she said that she didn't like was "Adam Bede", which is probably why I never read it. I have sometimes wondered how many of these books were first editions and what happened to them.

One day when I was at junior school, aged about nine, there was a discussion in the classroom about whether any of us might be related to a famous person. Because my surname was Cook, everybody hoped that I might be related to the Captain Cook who discovered Australia; sadly for them, I wasn't. "Well are you related to anyone famous?" they asked. So I told them that my great grandmother was cousin to George Eliot, whereupon our teacher remarked that it was a pity that I didn't take after that side of the family. Squelch!

When I was staying with my grandparents at a weekend, I would be allowed to stay up late on the Saturday evening to listen to a variety or music hall programme on the radio, if there was something suitable on it. Gracie Fields was the main attraction for everybody at that time. Although I never really liked her, I never said so. I thought that she had a harsh voice and I didn't find her comic songs at all funny. But, heigh ho, I got to stay up late! There was a chap called Harry Lauder who sang Scottish songs who was very popular too. I do remember one act that I liked called "The Western Brothers, Kenneth and George". They had upper-crust accents and drawled their way through their performance without pausing unduly for laughter or applause. I now realise that they were probably very polished satirists.

One of Grandad's brothers, my Great Uncle Billy and his wife Auntie Susie were usually staying with my grandparents at the weekends. Uncle Billy was a thin man with a rather lugubrious countenance and he was not known for either his generosity or his scintillating conversation. He owned a sweet shop in Sheffield but I don't recall him handing out any freebies, in fact he seemed the complete opposite of Grandad in both looks and character.

Amongst all the weekend newspapers was the News of the World. Uncle Billy and Auntie Susie bought this because it contained lots of competitions including a crossword puzzle that had so many alternative correct answers to the clues that it was not skill but pure luck if you picked the right one. Auntie Susie was born lucky and won a part share in the money prize most weeks. She also sometimes won the competition to select the winning fashions and put them in the right order. Occasionally Granny would pick up that newspaper and with a bit of rather shocked tut-tutting hastily put it down again. I don't think anybody ever bought the News of the World for the news value; it was strictly a scandal sheet of the most salacious kind.

Grandad and I used to inveigle Uncle Billy into playing solo whist, with Mother making up a reluctant fourth if she wasn't away in Bournemouth. He, poor man, did not have Auntie's luck and he would certainly have needed it playing against Grandad who had the gift of remembering every card that had been played and who had played it. We had a little box containing Spade Guineas, small round silvery discs, which we parcelled out between us and used for making bets. Playing for real money would never have been allowed as I think from something I overheard that Grandad's father had gambled away too much of the money he earned and his wife sometimes had a hard time making ends meet.

Grandad also had a sister called Cissie who was one of the few of his siblings who had survived into adulthood. She, poor soul, was prone to excruciating headaches, which were known as the "Whitworth Headache" as they had been passed down the generations. My grandad had them and to a lesser extent so did my mother. I remember seeing Grandad holding his head and saying in agonised tones, "Oh, Annie, my head does hurt". When I was very small I was once wheeled in a push-chair to visit Cissie who lived nearby. For some obscure reason I have a memory of her standing by a sideboard, showing Mother a new case of tea-knives which she had bought. I never saw her again but years later I learned that she had died from taking aspirins to ease the pain in her head. Aspirin was possibly the only drug available to her all those years ago. Lucky old me, I took after my father's side of the family and so far have escaped the Whitworth Headache. It was probably a migraine but that wasn't a word we knew at the time.

CHAPTER THREE

Because I spent so much time with my grandparents I got to know them very well, particularly Grandad. He used to take me to the cinema to see Shirley Temple films. For those of you who don't know who she was, she was an American child film star who could sing, dance and act from the age of about three. A pretty, curly-haired moppet, she eventually grew too big for the parts she played and of course she lost her lisp. Her two most famous songs were "Animal Kwackers in My Thoup" and "On the Good Ship Lollipop". Bless the girl, though, for when she grew up, she showed the world another side to her personality. She went into politics and was again famous as Shirley Temple Black and became a US Ambassador.

The Chesterfield football ground was only a couple of streets away from the back of my grandparents' home but we never heard any noise from it; there were probably enough trees around to deaden the sound. One Saturday afternoon Grandad took me to see a match there to the slight consternation of Granny who insisted that I should be well wrapped up in warm clothing as it was a bitterly cold day. She even suggested that a hot water bottle might be a good idea.

I don't remember the game, just the crowds as we left and Grandad saying, "Keep your elbows out and up" to ensure that I wasn't knocked over by the crowd as we left. There was no concern that there might be any clashes between the rival supporters. I don't think the crowds were unruly or violent in those days. We never went again. Neither my grandad nor my father was interested in football and I think that I was only taken for the experience, just as my father took me to a cricket match at his old school one time when Mother was away.

We sat with a lady who I hadn't met before but she and Father appeared to be friends. I was at one side of her and Father at the other. I wasn't very interested in the game and after a while I realised that I needed to go to the lavatory. I was quite a shy little girl and I found it increasingly difficult to tell the lady my problem. The longer you leave speaking up the more impossible it seems to get and the ever more urgent becomes your need. She must have realised what was wrong though because just in the nick of time she escorted me to the toilet. I suspect that everyone has embarrassing moments like that when they wish they could disappear off the face of the earth and those are the memories that tend to stay with you.

Grandad was always one for giving good advice but never talked down to you. One random piece of information was that pebble-dash on houses might cover a multitude of sins; maybe they might not be built of good quality bricks or there was a fault that was best covered over. Many years later, I was reminded of his words. We had gone to see a house that we thought we might buy and it had signs of subsidence. Knowing a little about such things, we suggested to the owners that their insurance might cover the problem. We ourselves had found another house more to our liking but the next time we were in the neighbourhood we saw that the offending wall had been pebble-dashed.

Another interesting facet of that house but not, I hasten to add, the reason why we did not buy it was that it had been haunted. The story was that the ghost of an old lady was sometimes seen, apparently searching for something. The house changed hands and the new owners found an ancient pair of spectacles which they placed in full view on the mantelpiece. From then on, the ghost was never seen again, presumably the spectacles were what she had been looking for and now she could rest in peace. A ghost story with a happy ending.

In later years Grandad told me that he had often regretted not buying some of the land to the rear of his property when he had the chance before the football ground was built. It wasn't that he wanted a large garden it was because he could have built stables there for his pony and trap and later turned them into garages, which would certainly have increased the value of his houses.

When I was very young, Grandad had a car but not for very long. It was a Wolsey and had what was called a dicky seat behind the front seats. That was where the children sat. There were no driving tests then and Father, who was an excellent driver, said he thought it was probably as well that Grandad soon got rid of his car as he would never be a good driver and he feared for his safety.

I have a memory of being in Grandad's car and Mother pointing to an orchard we drove past, saying it was Grandad's. Not the actual ground on which the trees were planted, she explained but the whole crop of apples for that year which he had bought in advance. This cut out the middleman or wholesaler but I suppose it could be a bit of a gamble as the crop might fail.

Now back to my relationship with Grandad. He owned a fruit, flowers and vegetable shop and also a stall for the weekly Saturday market. The stall was at the front of the market, on a corner, and looked so inviting with everything beautifully displayed, particularly the apples which had been polished with a cloth and shone with their wonderful reds, yellows and greens.

Once a year Chesterfield held a magnificent carnival which passed along the High Street then past the

Market Place so the front of Grandad's stall was the ideal place to stand and watch. We could sit on a chair, stool or upturned orange-box whilst waiting and then stand on it if we wanted to get a better view or someone stood in front of us.

The carnival went on for a long time, there were so many decorated floats – lorries that had woodland, seaside and all sorts of different scenes created on them and the names of the firms, charities or organisations sponsoring them printed on the sides or on banners. There were brass bands, children marching or dancing, clowns, acrobats, the Boys Brigade, Scouts, Girl Guides and Brownies, all smartly dressed in their uniforms. The clowns had collecting boxes and ran back and forth in front of the crowds, encouraging them to put their money in. People also tossed coins into the passing floats, some of which missed their target but were soon picked up by the clowns.

We don't have such large and elaborate carnival processions now, probably because of the insurance costs. Our culture has changed, claiming compensation has become a new industry. There are advertisements on television and in magazines and newspapers offering assistance in making claims, many saying "No win, No fee" to encourage us to sue. Years ago if you fell or hurt yourself, you were told, "Well you should have looked where you were going". Now the tendency is to blame somebody else, so it is understandable that all public spectacles or functions have to carry insurance.

Quite often I was taken around the wholesale warehouses where Grandad purchased his goods and these would be delivered to his warehouse. My opinion was occasionally asked on such weighty matters as to whether or not I thought that something would be a good buy. I remember saying that I thought that the pears were under-ripe and Grandad explaining how they would be just right by Saturday when they would be sold in the market; one had to allow the time for them to ripen without becoming over-ripe.

There were three wholesalers in Chesterfield: A.W. Mason's, Percy Mason's and Sir Ernest Shentall's. A.W. Mason never gave anything away. Percy Mason, who was thought to be a skinflint, sometimes cracked and gave me an apple or a penny or two. On an unlucky day with the first two, Grandad would say to me, "Let's go and see Sir Ernest and see what we can knock him down for." If Sir Ernest was there he would normally turn up trumps and once gave me a whole jar of sweets – lovely man! The Shentall Gardens in Chesterfield must have been named after him so I guess he was a public benefactor to all the townspeople and not just me.

The Shentall family had another claim to fame. I was told that their daughter Susan was spotted walking along the street by a film director. He decided she was exactly the person he wanted for his new film and persuaded her to act in it just as a one-off as she was not interested in a film career.

Percy Mason had a wife called Phyllis who had red hair that I later understood to be dyed. I got the impression, maybe wrongly, that she might have been "a bit fast" as the saying was in those days. I wasn't sure what that meant of course. Funnily enough the few people that I met later on in life who had red hair were called Phyllis, but I doubt if they were all "fast".

I'm sure my brother and Grandad were also good friends but at the time any of my adventures were taking place he would have been in Bournemouth with Mother. So his memories would all have been different.

A useful lesson which we both learnt from Grandad was the value of saving. We each had a children's saving account with Barclay's Bank and a Barclay's Bank money box. Barclays was on to a good idea with those boxes, as children would in all probability continue to use their bank when they grew up. I know I did. One day the advantage of saving some of our pocket money was shown to us in a practical way.

Grandad said, "If you each save up some money to pay for extra ice-creams or treats on your next summer holiday, I will double whatever you have saved." This sounded like a pretty good deal to me and I cut back on my expenditure. The day of reckoning came and Grandad was both surprised and gratified when he found that he had to cough up quite a few shillings to swell my holiday fund. My brother's philosophy was more a "spend as you go" one so I suppose it all balanced out and Grandad wasn't in danger of going broke over his rash promise.

CHAPTER FOUR

It was whilst walking with Granny to Chesterfield Railway Station as a small child that I saw a funeral procession for the first time. Black horses with plumes. Everybody stood still as a mark of respect as the procession passed and the men removed their hats and bowed their heads. Everyone wore a hat in those days. It was all very impressive otherwise I suppose that it wouldn't have stayed in my memory.

Although I don't recall the railway station in any detail, I do remember the stationmaster, who always wore a top hat, saying good morning to Granny. Then there was the guard, who waved a green flag to the driver to signal that all were safely aboard and we could go on our way. The guard was in charge of the Guard's Van and all the large trunks, cases, bicycles and anything else that was stored there for the journey. Only small items of luggage went into the racks above our heads. Below these luggage racks there were often pictures advertising holiday destinations with scenes of sea and sand and happy holiday makers, with the caption of "Come to Sunny Skegness" or wherever. The Guard would also patrol the train to make sure that all was well and to look in on any children who were making the journey alone "in the care of the Guard".

Some of the older trains did not have corridors and access to the compartments from the station platform was by a door with a window. To exit from the train you lowered the window by means of a leather strap so that you could reach the handle outside and open the door. Ladies tended to ensure that they travelled by a corridor train for obvious reasons. There were however "Ladies Only" compartments on non-corridor trains. A long journey without access to a loo would have been worry-some I imagine but perhaps the non-corridor trains were only used for short journeys.

As children our holidays were always spent in Bournemouth and we would travel there by train from Chesterfield. This entailed crossing London by taxi from St Pancras Station to Waterloo Station. I can still remember the excitement of that large, busy but not overcrowded station. The big joy was the News Theatre on the forecourt where we sat and watched not just the news but wonderful cartoons whilst waiting for our train.

We were never encumbered by luggage, as this was sent on in advance or possibly a porter was taking care of it. There were always uniformed porters at railway stations and if you needed one you stuck your head out of the train window and shouted "Porter". One would come rushing up and for a small tip would transport your luggage from the carriage or the guard's van to the taxi rank or the next train if you were continuing your journey.

I remember my excitement on my first trip to Bournemouth by train. I took my beloved teddy bear with me and told him that we would be travelling through the New Forest. I propped him up by the window so that he could have a good view. The New Forest had conjured up a picture of going through beautiful if somewhat frightening woods, possibly based on the forests of fairy tales. Alas it turned out to be nothing so exciting as my mental picture and the disappointment of being "let down" was never quite forgotten. Teddy and I were cheered up, though, by the sight of wild ponies. Nothing is ever all bad.

Bournemouth was a good holiday destination for children. You could paddle in the sea, make sand castles and dig moats and harbours to be filled up with buckets of water. This entailed mad dashes back and forth from the sea to refill the harbours before the last bucketful of water soaked through the sand and turned it into a dry dock.

If you tired of all these activities, you could go into the Gardens, an extensive area running more or less parallel with the sea. A stream ran through it and lots of boys and a few girls sailed their toy boats along its length. They rescued any capsized ones and helped them on their way with a pole or cane with a hook on the end. Fathers often joined in this activity which gave mothers a bit of peace. Squirrels played among the trees and like the birds were so tame that they too would eat out of your hand all the food that you could buy for them from the men who tended the gardens.

Mother's oldest and closest friend, Ida Tustin and her husband Jack lived in Bournemouth and they let us have the use of their beach hut. A boy called Alan occupied the neighbouring one with his mother; we never met his father who owned a hosiery and knitwear factory in the Midlands. Alan was the same age as my brother but a completely different type of boy. We found him irritating and what we called a "bit of a wet week".

Alan wouldn't stop teasing me until one day he carried on for too long and I whopped him one, whereupon he ran crying to his mother, claiming that I had broken his wristwatch. I thought I was in for trouble but his mother said, "Nonsense, you asked for it; you shouldn't have gone on teasing her." Alan always seemed to be on holiday at the same time as us and his mother and ours became good friends.

Years later when my teenage daughter Margaret and I were staying with Mother in Bournemouth, where she lived after Father died, Alan and his mother came for afternoon tea. If Alan had changed it was for the worse, not for the better. He had presumably inherited his father's business as he was now wealthy enough to have no need to work for a living. He devoted all his time to escorting his mother to coffee mornings, tea dances and visits to her friends. We shook hands and I wished that we hadn't – it was like holding a limp, wet fish that I felt might fall to the ground if I let go of it. He was so much more adept than I was at the tricky business of balancing a cup and saucer and a plate whilst eating a piece of cake that I couldn't imagine him leading any other sort of existence. I could sense Margaret, who had heard the story of how I made him cry, having a hard time suppressing a fit of the giggles.

Afterwards we told Mother that nobody could really be as awful as Alan so it must be his cover story for the fact that he was MI6 and a secret agent. Oh, how we wished we had kept quiet. Mother said, "Well, I wish that I had a son to take that much care of me" and we realise how sad it was for her that my brother had emigrated to Canada and never returned.

Apart from the annual ones to Bournemouth, my early train journeys were from Chesterfield to Sheffield and back with Mother and Granny. Ostensibly, these trips were made so that my hair could be cut by their approved hairdresser. Like so many little girls of my age and of that era I had short, straight hair and a fringe, so why nobody in Chesterfield was deemed competent enough to do the job was a mystery to me. I used the word "ostensibly" because we all enjoyed a day out in Sheffield and my haircut was a jolly good excuse.

At the salon, or whatever it was called in those days, I was plonked on a high stool or chair in front of a mirror. At least, there was privacy for this ordeal as all the clientele were dealt with in separate cubicles. I think these cubicles may have been curtained off from each other, rather like they are when having an examination in our local hospital or out-patients' department, but perhaps they were more permanent structures as I don't recall seeing or hearing other victims.

I was not normally a patient child and I found the whole performance irksome. The hairdresser was slow, incredibly slow, and I thought that I could do as good a job in half the time. Therefore, I announced my intention of becoming a hairdresser when I grew up. Granny said this was not a good idea: "Just think of all the heads of dirty hair you would have to wash to start with; I don't think that you would like that at all!" I considered the matter and was inclined to agree with her, but still felt drawn to being creative with a pair of scissors.

It so happened that some fifty or so years later, I was happily cutting my husband's hair and trimming his beard. Then my mother asked me to wash and set her hair when she could no longer get out and about easily and was not satisfied with her visiting hairdresser. A childhood ambition fulfilled.

Back to the fun part of our days in Sheffield. We travelled around the city by tram, something we didn't have in Chesterfield at that time. These were much more exciting than either buses or the trolley buses which were to replace the trams. Trolley buses were attached to overhead lines and I don't remember whether or not they needed tracks along the roadway. The direction of the trolley bus was reversed when it reached its destination by a man with a long pole shifting the connection in the same way that trains and trams could be re-routed by shifting the lines or points.

For me, the highlight of a day out in Sheffield was afternoon tea at a big department store that I think was called Cockaynes. There we sat on comfortable settees and chairs arranged around low tables. There must have been cakes or pastries but I don't remember them. I do, however, vividly remember eating lovely lobster sandwiches. Now there's opulence for you!

I used to while away my time on the train journey from Chesterfield by drawing patterns on a piece of paper and then colouring them in, usually in shades of brown and orange. The train would stop once on the way and the guard shouted out what I heard as "Dorinotly". I had forgotten this until I was looking at a map of the area quite recently and saw that Dore and Totley were two separate places on the way to Sheffield; that was what brought back the memory of my artistic endeavours.

Photo 1

Photo 2

Photo 3

1 Elizabeth Cholerton, my great grandmother.
2 My father's parents, Henry John and Alice Maria Cook.
3 My father, Maynard Cecil Cook, around the turn of the century, with his father.

Photo 4

Photo 5

Photo 6

Photo 7

4 Granddad Whitworth.
5 My mother, aged 17.
6 The boy soldier. My father in 1915.
7 Lieutenant M.C.Cook, Royal Flying Corps.

CHAPTER FIVE

Shopping in Chesterfield with my Granny was a leisurely affair. There were chairs at Woodheads grocery counters where one could sit and give one's "order" and either pay for the goods or, more often than not, it would be put on your account which would be payable monthly. If you paid cash, the bill and your money would be put into a container and hoisted up high to wing its way to an office high above your head. There it would be checked and the receipt and any change would be returned by the same method.

A similar process continues today in our local Tesco's when the checkout girl needs to clear surplus notes from the till. I watched as the notes from the till were put into a screw-top container, attached to a tube and promptly disappeared. Not nearly so much fun, though, as watching the criss-cross overhead lines of yore.

Before we started chopping down the world's trees to make packaging for just about everything, biscuits used to be in glass-topped containers in front of the counters and you bought or ordered 1/2 lb or so of whatever took your fancy, rather like being in a sweet shop with those lovely big jars of sweets and toffees, much more exciting for a child.

Shopping with Granny at Woodheads sometimes resulted in going home with a few hand-made chocolates. These were displayed on the counter in a glass cabinet and you could choose the ones you wanted from the assortment. There were violet creams and rose creams, each with a bit of crystallised flower on the top, and these were my favourites, these and the coffee creams. There were many others of course but I usually stuck with the same ones. You can find such goodies in the posher shops today but at a much higher price than they were then.

Quite often we would go upstairs with Mother to Woodhead's café which was divided into two sections. The first section had glass-topped tables made of cane or wicker. I associate these with tall glasses of milk and long chocolate biscuits that had a raised bit at each end of lovely extra thick chocolate. I still find that sort of table attractive – I wonder why? Usually, we sat in the second section, in seats that were in high-backed wooden booths, overlooking the High Street.

I can remember sitting in a window booth with Mother and her friend Monty Sadler when they were discussing a book by a new author called Agatha Christie. It sounded a funny name to me and I listened to their conversation – one of those rare occasions when my interest was not confined to my chocolate biscuit. Those window seats gave you a good view of what was going on below in the High Street, who was passing by and with whom. I bet that café was the fount of all the local gossip.

I learned later that Monty Sadler had lived opposite my grandparents' house on Tennyson Avenue until she married. Her father taught music to three generations of boys at the Grammar School and was known to all of them as Daddy Sadler. He was also known and disliked as a very strict disciplinarian and not averse to using the cane. Perhaps he was like that at home, too; if so, that would account for the fact that his wife was rather partial to a drop of whisky, which I am told she kept hidden in her wardrobe. Living with them was a tall, thin woman who was what was known as a "poor relation". Poor relations were given a home in exchange for duties as a companion and would often be taken advantage of as they had nowhere else to go. Life could be hard for a woman who was neither married nor had the ability to find suitable employment for her social position in life.

Shopping for new clothes could be an embarrassment as I don't remember ever being consulted as to my thoughts on the subject. School clothes were ok as one had no choice in the matter. I say "ok" but people of my generation will remember with retrospective horror those navy blue knickers, some of which had a pocket in them. A pocket was good as it meant that you didn't have to stick your hanky up your knicker leg. We did gym in our navy blue knickers; we must have presented a ghastly picture. I imagine this practice was stopped in co-educational schools, although I suppose the sexes were segregated for gym and games.

My worst memory is of a morning in town with, as usual, Mother and Granny. Suddenly they stopped at a shop they had never considered going into before. There in the window was a pretty dress of striped silky material, just about the right size for a little girl of nine, they must have thought. It was in shades of Mother's favourite flowers – sweet peas, whereas my favourite flowers were marigolds and nasturtiums and those lovely large white moonpenny daisies. I had a favourite dress that was yellow with lovely clover shaped yellow buttons and it is the only other item of clothing that I can remember at that age. Pretty dresses just aren't me and never were.

To my horror, the dress in the window was my size and Granny bought it for me. I think I must have succeeded in hiding my feelings because I don't remember being ticked off for looking sullen and ungrateful but I always tried my best to avoid wearing it.

A few years later I had another horrific clothes experience at the hands of Mother and Granny. A tailoress who I cannot recall, was given the task of making a skirt and jacket for me. It was light blue and I remember standing forlorn and resentful whilst having a final fitting. My embarrassment was intense and just when I thought nothing could get worse, it was decided that I should wear a hat with this outfit. I can only hope that this fit of madness on Mother's part was because of some function which we had to attend, but if it was then all memory of it has mercifully been banished from my mind.

I now wonder why in those days I never voiced my opinion on such matters. Possibly they were a sort of "fait accompli". Certainly I held quite strong opinions on some things and stated them clearly when given the opportunity. Perhaps it was just that my brother and I were brought up never to be knowingly ungracious or hurtful.

People did not have as many changes of clothes then as they do nowadays and they were divided up for the different seasons of the year. There would be a spring suit or costume as it was sometimes called, an autumn one and a few summer and winter dresses, plus of course jumpers or blouses to go with the suits. I'm sure the weather must have been far less changeable then. I know it is said that we only remember the warm, sunny days of the past but I do know that when the school summer term began after Easter our uniform changed from gymslips to summer dresses and we wore a blazer outside if it was chilly. We must have worn raincoats if it rained of course.

Granny did not have a great interest in clothes or window-shopping so she, usually with Mother in tow, would visit Mabel Hartley if there was something she needed. This was an upstairs emporium with chairs and settees on which you sat while the formidable Mabel Hartley displayed garments which she thought that you would like and which she considered would suit you. You then tried them on and made your selection. Mother didn't buy her clothes there. I think that they would have been out of her price range. However, I was with them both on one occasion when Granny bought Mother a lovely, slightly swing-back coat. It was a beautiful blue, which I was told was "French Navy" and she wore it for many years. Mabel Hartley's clothes never seemed to wear out, nor did they ever look out of date. But then, they were "classics" and not the latest high fashion.

CHAPTER SIX

Grandma Cook must have died when I was quite young because I have no more memories of her, either before or after realising that we did not like each other. What I do remember is that we went to live in her home in Queen Street after her death, presumably to look after Grandpa Cook. Their house, which was older and even larger than our house in Tennyson Avenue, was only about three or four minutes' walk away and John and I were involved in the move to the extent that we walked there with Robbie and we each carried something to take to our new home – to make us feel part of it all, I suppose. A good idea, I think, because I know I felt quite excited about the whole thing.

Another excitement was that we now had a dog. She was supposed to be a Scottish Terrier and was a sort of black colour, and her ears didn't stand up properly.

She was rather old and overweight and as soft as butter. I am not sure whether she had belonged to my grandparents or to Violet, who was Grandma's cook. I know she spent as much time as she could in the kitchen, which could account for her weight problem. Her name was Smut which somehow suited her.

Smut was well known for always having the last word: speak to her, and she grunted at the end of your sentence; she could always keep it up longer than you could. When Violet left Smut went with her; they were devoted to each other. There was also a black cat in the household when we arrived, but a new home had to be found for it rather quickly as it triggered off John's asthma attacks.

These attacks were frightening to listen to as John wheezed and gasped for breath. There seemed to be nothing that could be done to help apart from a solution of Friars Balsam in hot water in his bedroom for the steam to act as an inhalant. I remember lying in bed one night when he was having a particularly bad attack and being terrified that he was going to die. John was allergic to feathers as well as cats so he had to be propped up on flock-filled pillows and he couldn't have a feather-filled eiderdown to keep him warm in bed. There weren't the inhalers that we have today that can be carried around with us in case of need.

Smut was not the first dog in Mother's life. After the war ended in 1918 Father was living in Nottingham and during a visit to Chesterfield met my mother

again and promptly fell in love with her. On his
return to Nottingham where he was training to be a
master tailor, he sent her a present. It was rather a
shock when she found her present was a little King
Charles spaniel. Father was fond of all animals and
tended to assume that other people were, too. In this
instance he was right, both Mother and my
grandparents were completely won over by it. The
only other animal in their lives until then had been
Tommy, a rather intransigent pony who pulled the
trap and did his best to tip my great-grandmother out
when she climbed aboard. She was apparently a
stalwart soul and quite enjoyed the experience.

There was a strict rule about travelling in a pony and
trap. If you came to a steep hill, the able-bodied got
out and walked up it to save too much strain on the
pony. When I grew up and went abroad on holiday
and saw how some of the donkeys and horses were
treated, I was horrified. How, I thought, could all
those large, fat holiday-makers climb aboard and let a
poor, underfed-looking animal carry them up and
down hilly roads. I'm happy to say that times have
changed and most such animals today look well cared
for.

The next purchase my animal-loving Father made was
not so well received. He arrived home carrying a
monkey which he had bought on impulse from some
strange man, possibly thinking that it needed a good
home. He was told in no uncertain manner by my
mother, "You can take it back right now. If that
monkey stays, I go!" Come to think of it, if he hadn't
made the choice he did, I wouldn't exist – a sobering

thought.

I vaguely remember Grandpa Cook as being tall, and I know his bedroom was next to mine because I once saw him come out of it in his dressing-gown. I have no more memories of him until he went to Matlock Hydro. Matlock was a spa not far from Chesterfield, and the Hydro may well have been a nursing home. I realise now that he must have gone there because of his failing health and I assume that he died there. I remember there was a fountain in front of the building and I sat on the edge of it whilst my parents went in to visit Grandpa. Robbie must have been looking after me because I would never have been left anywhere on my own.

We continued to live in Queen Street until I was six or seven years old. We had a playroom, and my brother had a train set on a large board which could be lowered down from the wall. I can still see in my mind's eye a large armchair and a low window. Once I climbed through the window into the garden so it must have been low. The garden was large, and there were three lawns divided by two paths, each of which had rose-covered archways down its length. One of the lawns had a snowball tree in the middle which I loved; I can't think why I never had one when I had a garden of my own. Perhaps it was better to keep the memory, the reality may not have been quite so wondrous.

The hallway of the house must have been quite big because I used to skip up and down it. There was a table against the end wall with a telephone standing on it. This must have registered with me because I would have had it in my sight so often whilst skipping. Mother's grand piano was in the drawing-room, and this holds another memory for me. I was on the floor, underneath the piano, as usual, and my mother and brother were there, too – although not on the floor! – when a parcel arrived. Inside was a gift for each of us children from some friend or relative of my mother. I know we were told who she was at the time but it didn't mean anything to me. My present was a book entitled "Little Women", and it was far too old for me. My disappointment was all the greater on finding that my brother's present was a box of chocolates.

In the fullness of time, I either read "Little Women" or was force-fed it. I disliked it intensely! This may have been because I would so much have preferred to have received the chocolates. I do know that a few years ago, I re-read this wretched thing as a member of a book club. Sorry, Louisa M. Alcott, but I couldn't find a redeeming feature in your book. I suppose I wasn't reading it objectively and somehow I couldn't relate to any of the characters; they all seemed so good.

Nurse Gregory now replaced our beloved Robbie. She had previously been looking after a child called Thelma, whose father was either the manager or the owner of a couple of theatres in Sheffield. According to Nurse Gregory, Thelma was a very good little girl and I remember being taken to her home where we lay side by side on the floor, reading comics. She read all the words printed in the boxes beneath the pictures whereas I just read the bits in the bubbles emanating from each character's mouth, which, along with the picture, told me all that I needed or wished to know. It seems that I could always find a short-cut when it came to brain-work.

We were taken to see performances of Peter Pan and of a play called "Where the Rainbow Ends" at Thelma's father's theatres. Peter Pan was fine, and we all dutifully shouted "Yes" when asked if we believed in fairies, whether he did or not. I cannot remember the storyline of "Where the Rainbow Ends", but it was very sad and weepy. Maybe it was that experience that has prevented me ever going to see anything sad, however good people have told me that the show or film is. We sat in a Box which I thought was rather stupid as one's view of the stage at the far side was quite limited. It was considered rather special to have a Box and admittedly if you are a child or on the short side it is an advantage to have nobody sitting in front of you. I have sometimes wondered if the appeal of a Box is that it might give the occupant a sense of being important.

My only other memory of Nurse Gregory's reign is that we were given a boiled egg for breakfast every morning. I don't think that this ever bothered me but it irked my brother so he decided I should complain to Mother – a fine example of loading the gun and getting little sister to fire it. However, our breakfast menu became more varied and there were no repercussions.

When I grew up, I thought that Nurse Gregory had

probably been a rather lonely soul in need of love or affection. I knew that she was once in bed with me – I don't know why and it was only that one time – and she wanted to cuddle up close to me. I remember pulling away from her and feeling sorry for her as I did so.

It was while we were living in Queen Street that I first heard of the social divide of "Them and Us" that was prevalent at the time.

John and I had clambered up onto the flat roof of what I think was the garage, and a group of children from the Elementary School came along the road and started jeering at us and calling us names. We shouted back and a slanging match ensued and developed into both sides hurling missiles at each other.

Father must have heard the hullaballoo. He arrived on the scene, the children ran away and we were given a lecture. He told us that apart from our behaviour being unacceptable we were taking an unfair advantage. He explained that if the police or someone in authority had seen what was going on, the other children would probably have been the ones to take the blame as we lived a fairly privileged life and they came from a poorer district. He said that this was totally unfair of course and so we should take care never to put others at a disadvantage.

As I grew up, I realised how right my father was. I noticed that if a group of university students caused a disturbance or pushed each other into the river, it was referred to in the Press as "high spirits"; local lads from the wrong end of town behaving in the same way were "hooligans". This distinction has faded somewhat today, possibly because there are so many more university places, open to all and sundry, and the war was also probably a good leveller.

Now that we were living in Queen Street, I spent more time with Father. The countryside could not have been too far from our house as I remember him taking me for a walk and pointing with his stick to a field, telling me that the crop growing there was barley. He also knew the names of the birds we saw on our outings. I also remember Mother being quite cross with him one day because she said he had made me walk too far. Once he took me with him to Chatsworth House, the home of the Duke and Duchess of Devonshire, when he went there to measure the Viscount for a new suit. I was shown into the nursery to play whilst he was busy, but the only clear memory I have is of a wonderful horse.

A few years ago, Margaret and I took a short break holiday to Buxton in Derbyshire, and one of the included trips was to Chatsworth House. To my great joy, the rocking horse was still there. The tour of the house was pretty exhausting but we were able to have tea and relax in the gardens afterwards.

When I was about six or seven, Mother, John and I left Queen Street and went to live in Bournemouth for some months, possibly a year, for reasons I neither knew nor cared about; one just took life as it came. It must have been a fairly long period because

I went to school there.

We lived in a cottage in the grounds of a large empty house and we children had the run of the garden. A Mrs Jackson – Nurse Jackson to me – did the cooking and to some extent looked after us. I think she was supposed to take me to school, but one day she left me at the bus stop without giving me the penny for the bus fare. I can feel the desperation now as I called "Nurse! Nurse!" after her, to no avail. A lady asked me what was wrong and gave me my bus fare. I never told my mother. Maybe that experience is why I occasionally have worrying dreams involving buses.

Mrs Jackson had a son at boarding school and he spent his summer holidays with us. This is fixed in my mind because one day he and John were play-fighting with canes and I, ever protective of my brother, was afraid he might be losing and so entered the fray. They joined forces and chased after me, brandishing their canes. I ran to the open kitchen window and started to climb through; Mrs Jackson pushed me back and closed the window. That was two strikes against the woman; I never liked or trusted her again.

When I grew up, I understood the reason we spent all that time in Bournemouth. Grandpa had died and Father was clearing up his affairs. Grandpa was a gentle, kindly man who had paid for pension funds for many of his staff who had retired. This was a financial drain on his resources and he had mortgaged his house to help pay for them, so there was a hefty mortgage to pay off when the house was sold. Add to this, that the great Wall Street crash of 1929 had led to the dreadful depression in Britain in 1930 and 1931 and you can understand that the Cook family fortunes underwent a massive change. Money was tight and businesses were struggling. Hence, my mother left Father to attend to all this and salvage what he could whilst she lived in her beloved Bournemouth. I think it was likely that Granddad Whitworth paid for the services of the dreaded Mrs Jackson. He had a touch of the possessiveness and protectiveness of his daughter that sometimes gave rise to an element of mutual resentment between Granddad and my father.

We returned to Chesterfield and lived for a short while in a smaller house than hitherto. I remember my father asking me if I thought we still needed someone to look after us. My answer was "No, of course not". Mother hated the house, saying that John's bedroom was damp and making his asthma worse, so we moved a mile or two out of town to Brookside, an area verging on the countryside. My lifestyle there was idyllic: dens in the hedgerows, damming the brook, making bows and arrows and playing cowboys and Indians. Poor old John was often confined to bed in the wintertime which must have been pretty galling for him. If he resented his younger sister's good health and freedom it would be understandable but, in fact, he never showed any resentment to me. Like most older brothers, he tended to ignore my presence.

CHAPTER SEVEN

I had my first and very brief romance when I started kindergarten at St Helen's. The teacher was standing in front of a blackboard with squares on it and drawing Mickey Mouse using the squares as a guide. I think we were supposed to be doing the same in our exercise books. My page remained blank as did that of the boy sitting next to me. We were only interested in each other and we were busy chatting away happily when the teacher realised what was going on. She separated us and blighted our budding friendship. I wonder where that boy is now; indeed, I wonder if he is still alive, probably not as men don't usually live as long as us women.

St Helen's was an old school in what may have been two houses as there were two staircases. There were trees in the garden where we played and when a teacher rang a bell we would all line up two by two to go back inside. Miss Easterby was the Head Mistress. She is memorable because she once went to tea at the home of my friend Betty. Betty told us that they had had jelly and Miss Easterby had eaten hers with a fork, which we found fascinating and excruciatingly funny.

Betty had a claim to fame in that she always won the book race on junior sports day. This race was similar to the egg-and-spoon race in that you have to proceed carefully with a book balanced on your head. Betty had what could be called an unfair advantage as she had an almost flat top to her head and her hairstyle was such that it seemed to form a natural nest; certainly no book ever fell off Betty's head as she raced to the finishing line.

My best bet was the obstacle race. I was small for my age but quite tough and wiry and I could run, jump and wriggle around, through and over almost anything. However, I got my come-uppance well and truly one sports day. I was way ahead in the obstacle race and winning seemed certain until I came to the last obstacle and was faced with a large trough of water containing apples. I was expected to sink my teeth into one of these and head for the tape with it in my mouth. Putting my face under water and bobbing for an apple was something that I was quite incapable of doing. Consequently, it was not just a case of "and the first shall be last" it was "and the first shall never get there at all". I think I must have been about 30 years old before I was able to put my head under water voluntarily whilst trying to swim the width of the local baths.

There were four forms in the school: Kindergarten, Transition, 1st Form and 2nd Form. In Transition we chanted out times tables until we knew them off by heart. We also learned the Kings and Queens of England by the same method. First and 2nd Form work involved learning English grammar, nouns, pronouns, adjectives and adverbs, etc. and then parsing and analysis. We were also introduced in History lessons to Boadicea, King Alfred and King Canute and in Geography to tracing maps. I still associate oranges with Jaffa in present day Israel; at that time it was Palestine as Israel had not been created then. We enjoyed pin-pointing on our maps where different things came from.

I don't remember there being any boys after Kindergarten; presumably they went to a school for little boys before going to the Grammar School, which incidentally was an old Elizabethan grammar school. At the age of nine, we girls graduated to the Girls' High School, which we had all referred to as "The Big School" when we were at St Helen's. It was a modern school by comparison with St Helen's and it had been built next door to the boys' grammar school – something that was no doubt appreciated by the older pupils. We left Chesterfield when I was twelve, so I cannot speak from personal experience, but I do know that there was one section of the wall dividing the two schools which always seemed to be in need of repair; it was from this vantage point that I once watched a game of rugby until I was hauled away. I thought how unfair it was that girls were not taught the game as it was obviously much more fun than netball.

Tennis was the sport our school was noted for. We had six grass courts and three hard courts. I was told that several pupils had gone on to be Junior Wimbledon players but I cannot vouch for the truth of this. Our other claim to local fame was the quality of the plays which the senior girls put on each year in our large Assembly Hall.

The Assembly Hall had a beautiful parquet floor which I really loved. In fact I found the whole building both impressive and friendly at the same time. It was in the hall that I discovered what was to me one of the strange and amusing facts of life. It must have been Prize Day or some such function because the Hall was full of people. Margaret Wilson, a very pretty little girl with short, tightly-curled hair, like that in Gainsborough's Blue Boy painting, grabbed me by the hand and tried to pull me through the crowd. The crowd parted for her and the women cooed sickeningly over Margaret's beautiful hair. Then they closed ranks and I was left being dragged along in her wake. Short, straight hair with a fringe does not open many doors for you but it does spare you the horror of being petted and pawed over by strange women.

I often felt sorry for Margaret. We were supposed to be friends because our mothers had known each other for many years. Her father had been a doctor and had died before I knew her. Margaret was looked after by Fanny, who was the general factotum and even more protective of her than was Mrs Wilson. If there was a tea party at her house we were entertained by a Charlie Chaplin or Laurel & Hardy film. That

63

was fine; the only trouble was that Mrs Wilson owned a cine camera and we had to sit through what seemed an endless series of shots of Margaret playing or dancing or enjoying her annual holiday in Jersey before we got to them. I used to feel embarrassed for Margaret, quite needlessly I realise on reflection as it never seemed to bother her at all; she was used to it. There was a big folding screen by the drawing room door which was almost entirely covered by photographs of Margaret so she was constantly on display.

We went to the same dancing classes where we did ballet and tap. We usually had to perform a tap dancing routine together at the Annual Show, in addition to any solo performances. We both had elocution lessons; Margaret, poor girl, was made to practice this and her dancing in front of a large mirror, whereas I wasn't pressured into anything at all. As well as this, Margaret had singing lessons to contend with – all that and homework, too; no wonder I pitied her. And, "Oh, yes" she informed us solemnly, "I have to have my hair brushed with one hundred strokes every night at bedtime". I think she could have claimed extreme provocation if she had done her mother and Fanny a serious injury.

Another magnificent feature of our building was the Gymnasium. It was beautifully equipped with wall bars, vaulting horses and much more. For me, the greatest delight was the number of climbing ropes. You could climb up two adjacent ones, put your arms through the gap then spread them out. This was called "Flying Angels" and the nearest thing I ever got to being angelic.

The Headmistress of this excellent school was Miss Hyslop, a woman I remember with gratitude for her understanding. One day I put my hand up to be excused and was given permission to go to the loo, which was situated in the cloakroom. In the cloakroom were some horizontal rails and I thought I would take advantage of this and do some somersaults on them. From my upside down position I became aware of Miss Hyslop looking down at me. "I think you should go back to your form room now, Margaret," she said in a kindly tone. Thus, she gained a respectful and obedient pupil, something a ticking-off would probably not have done.

There was only one teacher who had an adverse effect on my life. She arrived on the scene as our new singing mistress when I was eleven or twelve years old. She was tall and thin and had a very high soprano voice whereas I was a contralto. I enjoyed singing and was even in the House choir the year we won the Singing Bowl.

One day we were all singing en-masse, "Where'er you walk, cool gales shall fan the glade, trees where you sit shall crowd into a shade". It was a song which I liked very much and still do but it contained one very high note, quite beyond my range. The wretched woman made me stand out in front of everybody and sing that note. I tried and tried and eventually made it. She then angrily berated me for not having succeeded in the first place, it showed that I hadn't been trying.

I was so humiliated and hurt at the injustice that from then on I always mimed and never sang again.

My singing life was not entirely destroyed, though. Long journeys in the car with my children were enlivened by the sound of us belting out raucous renditions of "She'll be coming round the mountain when she comes", "Clementine" and irreverent versions of "The Battle Hymn of the Republic". I recall John Brown's Body having a pimple on its bum amongst other things while his soul went marching on.

I realise now that I was very stupid to have allowed one silly woman to destroy my confidence and put a stop to my singing. I had a school-friend who came from a musical family and sometimes we would all stand around the piano at her house and sing. One day Joyce's mother told me that I really should enter the individual singing competition at school. I didn't of course because I would have died of embarrassment singing a solo, but it was nice to know that someone thought that I was good enough to try.

Every time I shake a duster out of a window I take great care as I remember that Joyce's mother was doing just that very thing when she leaned out too far and followed it to the ground. It must surely have been a downstairs window or else she landed on a convenient bush as when I knew her she seemed hale and hearty.

It was my friendship with Joyce that had led to my having elocution lessons. She had a strong

Derbyshire accent which I had picked up without realising it and it wasn't long before Mother sought to remedy this and packed me off to elocution lessons after school. This was fine by me. I could mark the words with the necessary inflection signs and pauses etc. in no time at all and learn it off by heart as I walked back to school that evening. I even passed the grading exams with either distinction or honours, until it came to the Bronze Medal when I learned that it was to be a public affair. Just as I had with the Brownies, I dug my heels in and said that I didn't want to do this anymore. My words, if I remember rightly, were, "I'm sorry but I have no intention of spouting in public." Mother, having, as she said afterwards, seen me go ashen when I was told that the exam would be in public, agreed. However, I did get severely told off for using the slang term "spouting" instead of "performing" or "reciting".

I enjoyed poetry and was quite happy to recite it at school although it did seem that I was a little out of step with some of my form-mates when it came to making individual choices. Three of my favourites were:

Ariel's song from the Tempest

"Full fathom five thy father lies;

Of his bones are coral made;

Those are pearls that were his eyes:

Nothing of him that doth fade,

But doth suffer a sea-change

Into something rich and strange.

Sea-nymphs hourly ring his knell:

Ding-dong.

Hark! now I hear them – ding-dong, bell."

and William Blake's

"Tyger, Tyger, burning bright

In the forests of the night …"

And, of course, my first love, the verses of the Rubaiyat of Omar Khayyam.

We were introduced to Shakespeare's plays at an early age by a lovely soft-voiced English mistress, Miss Rowe. We discussed and read them out loud and took it in turns to enact scenes from "A Midsummer Night's Dream" and, after that, "The Merchant of Venice". I had to write out Portia's "The quality of mercy is not strained" speech umpteen times as a punishment for some misdemeanour, so for years I could recite it faultlessly.

CHAPTER EIGHT

Among my worst early memories are tea parties. You had to wear a pretty dress for a start. Sandwiches filled with gristly ham or with hard-boiled egg and wisps of cress, which somehow managed to escape from one's mouth, and jelly and lumpy pink blancmange are what I recall with horror. There would be a paper serviette that one either lost or fiddled with until it was in shreds, leaving you wondering what to do with it. Another source of worry: could one perhaps hide the gristle in the serviette? No, not if it had been torn to shreds!

If, like me, you had been taught to finish up what was on your plate, you felt embarrassed when as soon as your plate was empty, a grown-up, thinking that you might still be hungry, pressed more food upon you. Another gristly sandwich was the last thing you wanted. You had to finish up what you had; you could hardly leave food, however unpalatable, on your plate and then dive into the cakes and biscuits.

I think that there must have been social or business reasons for my attendance at some of these tea parties because the children giving them were often not my friends and were a little younger than I was, but we did go to the same dancing class. The two I remember were Margaret Malsom and Margaret Swale. They were cousins and brought there by what looked to me like a couple of ancient aunts. I wonder if they are still alive; not the aunts of course!

The dancing class was run by a middle-aged lady who had been a professional dancer. I think it was part of the Rotherham School of Dancing and was well known for the annual performances which they gave both there and in Chesterfield. This rather forceful woman had two beautiful twin daughters, or perhaps they were her younger twin sisters. I think they were also professionals and I still remember a dance they did one year for our show. There was a flimsy curtain across the stage, dividing them, and as one danced in front of it and the other behind it, they gave the impression of a dancer and her shadow. Obviously, it must have called for perfect coordination between them.

I was never worried or embarrassed at performing on the great day of our show. It was the dress rehearsals that floored me. They took place in the cold, harsh light of day, with none of the sense of anonymity one got from a darkened auditorium. Odd friends and relatives would turn up to watch and, you felt, compare you unfavourably with their own little darlings. This was ok as far as ballet dancing was concerned as I was the only local child to do a solo turn and so had no rivals. The most ghastly dance was one in which I had to be John Peel, as in the Scottish folk song, "Do ye ken John Peel", leading lots of little tots galloping around the stage being his horses and hounds. I knew it would be "all right on the night" but I turned sullen and awkward at rehearsing in front of the Ancient Aunts and their contemporaries and was tempted to refuse to dance ever again; but cowardice got the better of me and I chickened out.

Another cause for rebellion was a tap dance double act with Margaret Wilson, she of the pretty face and curly hair. The tap dancing was fine but the act involved singing a song, "The Lily of Laguna", which would doubtless not be considered politically correct today as the young couple in the song were black Americans dressed in cotton-picking type clothes. The song goes something like this:

"She's my lady love

She's my dove, my baby love

She's no girl to sit around and dream

She's the only queen Laguna knows.

I know she likes me

I know she likes me

Because she says so

She's the lily of Laguna

She is my lily and my rose."

As I was the plain Jane, I was supposed to take the boy's part and do the singing. No way! We swapped roles. As my father told his mother, "You try making my daughter do something she doesn't want to do."

I call myself the "plain Jane" because when I was a child the ideal was to have curly hair and a pretty if somewhat characterless face and behave in a rather more restrained and ladylike manner than I could ever achieve. But I reckon that I had a lot more fun in life than the Margaret Wilsons of that world.

Tea parties as such became less frequent as you grew older; perhaps there is an age when these things die a natural death. You were now invited to tea from time to time at the homes of your friends and they in turn would come and have tea at your house, but these were informal affairs and you were treated as part of the family.

Many of these activities were curtailed with the advent of war and anyway we had already left Chesterfield and moved to Swansea by then. The dancing class there was a dull and uninspiring affair and I was tired of sore and sometimes bleeding toes as I teetered on the points of my ballet shoes so I was more than happy to give it all up at the age of 15.

I had by then lost my Derbyshire accent but I don't suppose it was long before I picked up a Welsh one.

My brother never picked up any local accents nor did he acquire a Canadian one in spite of living in that country from 1947 to the end of his life in 1986. So now there were no more dancing or elocution lessons and it was rather a relief as none of my new friends in Wales were subjected to these. I imagine the Welsh would never have considered trying to eradicate their national accent. I don't think Mother liked me speaking in anything other than the standard BBC English type of voice, but maybe I now merged in with the accents she heard every day and she ceased to notice.

CHAPTER NINE

After we moved from Chesterfield town centre to Brookside I still spent a great deal of time with Granny and Grandad Whitworth as I lived with them when Mother was away from home, although her absence was not now such a frequent event. I was about eight or nine years old I think and quite capable of travelling to and from school with other local children but it was very convenient to have lunch most days of the week at my grandparents' house. The majority of the children who had to travel to school had school dinners – I was spared that horror!

My friend Ruth had a bicycle and she would call for me after lunch and we would return to school together. Sometimes, I would sit on the saddle whilst she stood on the pedals. All illegal of course, like riding on pavements, but nobody took any more notice of that than they seem to do today. One lunchtime on the way back to school, I vividly remember turning my head towards a house at the end of the street we were cycling down and seeing flames engulfing a downstairs room. I yelled out, "There's a fire!" and a man ran across the road towards the house. Ruth pedalled on and presumably the man took action. I never knew the outcome and I certainly never heard of any great disaster; the house seemed ok when we next went by. There were many times later when I wondered if we children should have done more than just pass by, although I cannot think what we could have done.

Life at Brookside was much more free and easy than it could ever be in a town. The countryside was on the doorstep. Well, actually, that is not true; it was at the end of the garden. A hop over the fence and you were at one end of the High School hockey pitch. My brother used to watch the girls playing from his bedroom window when he was considered too poorly to go to school. Turn to your left and you were in a hayfield and from there you could walk past an orchard and down to the Brook. There was a ghastly sight on the way, possibly designed to deter anybody thinking of scrumping the apples; it was a double row of wires with dead birds hanging from them. More likely, of course, it was a warning to other birds as to what would happen to them if they pecked at the apples. I always ran past with my gaze averted.

It was in the hayfield that I experienced my first feeling of absolute peace and contentment. Standing in the field all by myself one day I was lucky enough to see a skylark descending to its nest in the long grass. So I lay down too and thought that, like the skylark, I was invisible to the rest of the world. As I lay there, looking up at the sky, I heard a gentle drone and saw a small aeroplane slowly crossing above my head. The sound, the sky, the skylark and the long grass filled my whole being with a sensation and wonderment that I would be hard put to describe. Little did I know that in a few years' time the sound of a plane would be so different and so menacing; unless of course it was "one of ours".

The little stream or brook that gave Brookside its name ran through a tunnel underneath the main road to Holymoorside. You could go down to this and hop from one side of the water to the other as you made your way along it, although if there had been a lot of rain it would prove rather hazardous. Beside the stream was a narrow path known as Lovers' Lane which linked up with Somersall Lane and a small playground with swings, see-saws and roundabouts.

The trolley bus terminal was across the road from the playground and it was there that we spent most of our Saturday pocket money in the Tuck Shop that was placed there to catch the bus passenger trade. I had a passion for whipped cream walnuts but had to remember not to eat them before we went to the playground. The swings were not too bad but a see-saw or roundabout would guarantee me promptly losing all that I had just consumed.

The house we lived in had quite a large rear garden with a rockery separating the well-tended half near the house from the "left-to-nature" half backing on to the hayfield. Lilac and laburnum and flowering cherry trees divided us from neighbouring gardens and there was an abundance of flowers, particularly roses and sweet peas, so it was a sweet smelling garden and there was always a constant supply of flowers for the house.

We now had a new dog called Jock. He was a Scottish terrier but unlike Smut, his predecessor, he was of uncertain temper. One day he bit my brother and was promptly got rid of. I hoped and imagined he went to a good home but my mother's view would have been that there could be no mitigating circumstances so she might have imposed a death sentence.

It wasn't long before my father arrived home with an Airedale called Roger. He was about 18 months old and I'm sure I was never told his history. Roger was loved by us all and by all who knew him. He was clever, gentle and fun and never known to be anything but friendly to people, other dogs and even cats, birds and rabbits. One evening my parents planted chrysanthemums all down the left-hand-side of the garden. Next morning they looked through the bedroom window and the plants had disappeared, nibbled down to the roots by Roger's rabbit friends.

Living nearby was a snappy, aggressive little fox terrier who used to growl at Roger and one day he made the mistake of attacking him. Roger knocked him down, stood over him and then walked away without a backward glance. I don't know what he said to him in dog language but it was certainly effective; the vicious terrier was a reformed character from then on. Many times in my life I have witnessed dogs silently communicating with each other and getting their message across. But as this is a record of childhood memories, I won't go into that now.

Father enjoyed gardening, provided it was a project. He did not like the weeding and general maintenance so he attacked weeds with a hoe and gave me the job of picking them up. I once suggested that we should swap over but he rejected the idea. Among his projects was a concrete base on which he built a superb dog kennel. Naturally, the dog never used it; he was happily living in the house and saw no reason to change his lifestyle. Another abortive project was the making of a pond at the side of the house. I seem to remember that it did not hold water. This was no surprise to Mother who never entered into the spirit of his bright ideas.

The real joy of the garden was the rockery at the front. There were standard roses near the house and then enormous rocks of different shapes, shades and sizes, and I would jump from one to another. There was one that we christened the Brazil Nut; this was my favourite but not easy to balance on. Saxifrage, arabis and all the many colours of aubrietia filled the gaps; there was also a lovely yellow plant that I can't remember the name of. Mother would come home from shopping sometimes with another little sixpenny potted rockery plant that she couldn't resist and somehow she would find a home for it.

On Sunday the Walls ice-cream man used to do his rounds, riding a bicycle which bore the message, "Stop Me and Buy One". The ice creams were in a big box on the front of the bicycle as far as I remember and I don't think I ever gave any thought as to how they were kept frozen. He had a bell which he rang to announce his arrival and to attract custom.

Regularly on a Sunday Roger would take up his position on the two largest stones on the high rockery at the front of the house, from which vantage point he could see and hear his friend the ice-cream man arriving. They would greet each other joyously and Roger would be given a free two-penny ice-cream, the sort that was sandwiched between two wafers. It wasn't because we were good customers; the Walls man knew that we usually made our own ice-cream for Sunday lunch.

I used to sit on the kitchen doorstep stirring the mixture halfway through the freezing process. We had no refrigerator of course so it was made in a double container, the outer one of which was filled with purchased ice and freezing salt. The inner one contained cream, also made by us from unsalted butter and milk in a small machine with a pump handle action. I don't know if there were any other ingredients. It all sounds laborious but the end product was worth it. Cream-making machines were in existence for many years after that.

Mother employed a girl called Lilian to help her in the house. Not only did Lilian do most of the housework, she also turned out to be an excellent cook, although she was only sixteen when she came to us. It sounds remarkably young but before the war most children left school when they were fourteen and went out to work. This was an improvement in social conditions as in Grandad Whitworth's childhood they could leave when they were only twelve years old. I was told that he left school at that age and got a job as an errand boy in order to help his mother financially because his father was in the habit of gambling most of his money away. Errand boys rode bicycles with large baskets in the front and delivered the contents to the customers' homes. I don't suppose that they were paid very much but if they were cheerful and helpful they would sometimes be given a tip.

Lilian was a rather plump, good-natured girl and she spent quite a lot of her spare time keeping John company when he was confined to his bedroom with asthma or bronchitis. Mother found this a great help, particularly in spring and early summer when she suffered badly from attacks of hay-fever. One Sunday Lilian invited me to her home for tea and I have never forgotten the experience.

Her father had been gassed in the First World War and at times could scarcely breathe. They lived in a small terrace house with no bathroom and her father slept on his hands and knees on a couch in the kitchen. He was unable to breathe if he lay down flat and he certainly would not have been able to climb the stairs to a bedroom. On his good days he managed to go out into the back garden where he grew prize-winning chrysanthemums.

I think Lilian's mother did some tailoring or dressmaking but I'm not sure that I have remembered correctly. She would not have been able to leave her husband for long enough to go out to work. The horrors that war can bring were clear to me at a very young age.

CHAPTER TEN

Now that we children were older and no longer had or needed someone to look after us, I got to know my mother much better and enjoyed being with her. We played card games, like Bezique, a game for two players, and a hilarious, noisy one called Pit, which I think was based on trading cereals on the stock market. The more players the better and the noise and laughter was exhausting. Mother taught me to knit and crochet and, best of all, she played the piano to me. Sometimes she would play Chopin, Liszt and Rachmaninov and sometimes it would be songs which we could sing or stories that she could tell to the music. Grieg was particularly good for this. Years later she would entrance my young daughter in the same way.

Mother was a very gifted pianist and it is a great pity that neither John nor I inherited her talent. She studied the piano under Dr Frederick Staton in Sheffield until the First World War intervened. When she was sixteen, Granny bought her a beautiful Steinway grand piano which she continued to play until well into her seventies. Both she and Father could sing, another talent neither I nor my brother inherited.

But both John and I always enjoyed listening to music, be it classical, musicals, jazz or popular music. John had piano lessons for a very short time; his health probably interfered with them and they soon ceased. I persevered for a while and then I gave up or more likely I was given up as a bad job. My problem was that although I knew all about FACE and EGBDF, sharps and flats, I was incapable of relating the musical score to the piano keys. The only one I could recognise and locate was G and to proceed further I used the method of the next note to be played being, say, a line and a space above or two spaces below and working it out from that. It was a form of dyslexia I suppose because I tried again when my daughter had a guitar and was just as unsuccessful.

It is strange the odd things that stick in one's mind. I was in bed recovering from some illness – chickenpox or measles – and Mother brought me my lunch on a tray. It was scrambled egg on toast. The tray had a pretty cloth on it and the egg was garnished with a sprig of parsley. Care had been taken. Mother scrambled the egg herself and made it all so attractive. I was suddenly very aware of being loved, something I had never thought about before.

Another memory of being ill and in bed is not a good one and destroyed my faith in our family doctor, Dr McGlashun. I was, and still am, particularly prone to gagging if anything is inserted into my mouth and in those days in order to peer down one's throat, a spatula was placed on the tongue to hold it down. It occurred to me that if I could train myself to hold my tongue completely flat then there would be no need for any spatula. After practising in front of a mirror I could and still can produce a perfect view of the back of my throat. I told Dr McGlashun of this and asked if he would let me show him. He agreed but as soon as I opened my mouth he shoved this lolly-pop type stick onto my tongue, whereupon I heaved and choked and he could not see a thing. Not only was I horrified that he had lied and deceived me but I thought how incredibly stupid he was. You will gather from his name that he and his partner Dr McCrae were Scottish. Just to show how easy it is for a childhood experience to colour one's judgement, I must confess that I have always had lurking at the back of my mind a wariness of Scotland and its inhabitants. I don't let this affect my relationship with anybody with Scottish ancestry because I am aware that it would be absolutely ridiculous for one incident alone to do this. Indeed, I have had several very close friends and a much-loved sister-in-law with Scottish antecedents. But it does make me realise that it's on small, seemingly insignificant incidents that prejudices can be based.

Naturally most of my life in Brookside was spent playing or exploring out-of-doors. All children in those days had so much freedom that has been lost today. So off we went after breakfast and managed to come home in time for lunch or tea. Sometimes we went on bicycles to more distant places and then possibly took sandwiches. I know we cycled to Holymoorside, not far away, because I used to copy the boys and come back down the steep hill to home with my feet on the handlebars – fortunately there was not a lot of traffic pre-war. My bike was smaller than anybody else's so I had to struggle to keep up with the others; however I developed very strong legs! We also went to Linacre Reservoir and Linacre woods and picked a few bluebells to take home tied to the handlebars of our bikes – only a few because they would soon droop and die and we were taught not to denude the countryside. Another flower that grew in some profusion was the cowslip; you don't see so many of these today.

My best friend in many of these exploits lived within signalling distance with a torch at night between her bedroom window and mine. To my shame, I find that I cannot recall her name. I do remember that her entire garden had been turned into a tennis court, both her parents being keen players and we children sometimes played too.

Strangely enough I do remember the name of another girl who lived nearby who was not a close friend but was in the same form as me. She was very tall, her name was Joan and her father was the Chief Constable. They lived in a lovely big house with a large garden and one year she invited me to their fireworks party. There was no rain and no fog which always seems unusual on 5th November. The fireworks were lovely and there was a good supply of sparklers for us to wave about but best of all was the huge bonfire, the special dark treacle bonfire toffee and at the end the potatoes baked in the ashes.

If this was the best party I had ever been to, the very worst was definitely the one I was invited to by a girl a couple of years older than me who also lived nearby. I knew none of the other girls and I felt so miserably out of place that I kept making mistakes in all the games we played. There was one game called "Turn the Trencher" which involved someone spinning a large plate and calling out a name. If it was your name that was called you had to catch the plate before it fell down. Failure resulted in the payment of a forfeit, usually embarrassing in nature. I was in such a bad state of misery and nerves by the time my name was called that I couldn't move. I just wanted to disappear into a hole in the ground and the shame and humiliation were unbearable. Perhaps it is not surprising that I still don't like large parties as they make me feel inadequate. Small dinner parties I can cope with and enjoy and coffee mornings aren't too bad because they don't involve a room full of strangers.

My brother also had friends living close by: Alan and Dennis Bird. Dennis was my age and Alan was two years older. I liked Dennis because he would happily include me in their games of Cowboys and Indians or Cops and Robbers and I particularly remember the two of us making little boats out of walnut shells and sailing them in the kitchen sink. I always thought that Alan didn't like me but many years later John told me that Alan had loved me. I guess the trouble with boys is that after a certain age they become too embarrassed to show their feelings and can come across as disliking one. It's encouraging to think that perhaps later on in life any fellow I fancied and who had ignored me might perhaps have been secretly in love with me. Well you can dream, can't you?

CHAPTER ELEVEN

I have no idea why we left Brookside and returned to live at no. 18 Tennyson Avenue; I may have been told at the time. The house was large and I don't remember it with any affection. I think we must have spent a Christmas there because I know I was encouraged to make presents for people as opposed to buying them. This I rather enjoyed and became quite creative for a while. This creativity didn't last for long which must have been a great relief to the recipients of my gifts.

The dining room was where these activities took place and it is the only room which I can remember at all clearly. Father would appear to have fallen asleep in the big armchair after Sunday lunch whilst listening to a symphony concert on the wireless. My brother would get me to crawl behind the chair and switch the channel to Radio Luxemburg. Always an unsuccessful manoeuvre as at the very last moment a voice would say, "Oh no you don't!" How much Father really objected to Pop music I don't know but he made it plain that he disliked Bing Crosby and his crooning until the appearance of the new boy on the block. Frank Sinatra was deemed even worse and suddenly Bing Crosby became more acceptable.

Although I missed the freedom of the outdoor life I had led at Brookside I was now old enough to be able to do other things. For example, I could go to Queen's Park or the cinema and I often went to stay with Betty, she of the flat head who always won the book race at junior school. She lived about seven miles away in the mining village of Doe Lea and I was treated as one of the family for many years.

Queen's Park was on the other side of the town and had a boating lake. I went there with John and a friend and spent my pocket money on hiring a rowing boat. John went home alone ahead of me, whereupon Mother asked him where I was. "Oh," he said, "When I last saw her she was going down for the third time, glug-glug." Mother was not amused and I was forbidden to go boating again. She couldn't be cross with me because nobody had told me not to and therefore I wasn't being disobedient.

Going to the cinema could be a hazard, too. John and I made up a foursome with Joyce Derbyshire and her brother to see "Things to Come", a film based on the book by H.G. Wells. I don't know what effect it had on Joyce but I had a terrible nightmare and must have cried out because Mother came into my bedroom to find me a shivering, quaking wreck. Bless her, she rallied round and brought me a drink of hot milk and soothed me off to sleep again. Films were strictly censored after that.

China and Japan were at loggerheads at this time and Japan must have been the aggressor because our sympathies were with China if I remember rightly. Certainly it was during this time that our school encouraged us to knit woollen squares to be made up into blankets for the Chinese. Knitting was something I could cope with as opposed to sewing. It was my lack of skill and my hatred of sewing that had led to me leaving the Brownies a year or so previously. I remember saying to my mother, "I don't mind jumping over their silly toadstool but I won't sit in a corner and hem stitch a handkerchief." Having witnessed my attempts with a needle and thread and knowing that I didn't enjoy being a Brownie she agreed that I could leave.

It may well have been my father's lecture at Queen Street on the unfairness of the "them and us" culture that gave rise to my interest in politics at the age of eleven in 1935 when there was a General Election. I told my father that I was all for Communism, that is, all people being equal and so on but I didn't think it could possibly work as there would always have to be those in charge and those who obeyed. He said that he had sometimes thought that we could do with a benevolent dictatorship but that wouldn't work either as dictators, once in power, ceased to be benevolent. No doubt he had Adolf Hitler in mind and also

Joseph Stalin, although I don't think that Stalin had ever been considered by anybody to have been benevolent.

My parents were Conservatives and I supported Labour, voicing my views to any of my schoolmates who might listen. Then I saw a Labour poster showing a signpost, one arm of which said "Armament" with an arrow pointing to "War". The other one said "Disarmament", pointing to "Peace" - at least that is how I remember it. Hang on, I thought, they've got that wrong. I visualised a playground where some children with sticks were attacking others who were defenceless. To my mind, the bullies might not be attacking if they knew their victims were also armed with sticks and could strike back.

I changed my allegiance and became a Liberal and mounted a new soapbox. What a pain in the neck I must have been! Incidentally, the Conservatives won, Stanley Baldwin became Prime Minister and I retired from the political scene.

The next big National Event was the death in December 1936 of King George V. His son the Prince of Wales became King Edward VIII but was never crowned. He had been headline news for some time because of his rather blatant relationship with Mrs Wallis Simpson, an American woman who had been divorced not once but twice. Divorce was not quite the norm it seems to have become today. I remember all this being about Christmas time because we children went around singing, "Hark the Herald Angels sing, Mrs Simpson's pinched our King."

Edward was told that although he could marry Mrs Simpson, she could not become Queen; it would be what is known as a morganatic marriage. This was not acceptable to the King so he made a speech to the nation, announcing his abdication. His brother, the then Duke of York and father of our present Queen Elizabeth, came to the throne as King George VI. So in the course of 1936 we had three different kings!

Edward and Mrs Simpson married in 1937 and lived in France. When the war started in 1939 some suitable role had to be found for Edward and he was appointed Governor of the Bahamas and they went to live in Nassau. After the War ended they returned to live in exile in France and we never saw them again, although I believe that he made one or two private visits to England to see his mother, Queen Mary the Queen Mother. It was perhaps as well that Edward abdicated as both he and Wallis Simpson had been friendly with and seemingly supportive of Adolf Hitler and that could have been a little awkward when we declared war on Germany.

Moving house was something that I was becoming used to. It was no big deal in those days. Father would draw a floor plan of each room and cut out pieces of paper to scale representing each piece of furniture which he would then happily shuffle around on the floor plan until he was satisfied that he had the perfect arrangement. He would then be able to direct operations with his usual precision. This did not stop him subsequently rearranging everything when the mood took him. Mother, on the other hand, never changed the position of anything at all if she could help it. The relaying of carpets was no problem as people did not have the luxury of wall-to-wall carpeting. They bought a standard size carpet of, say, 12 by 10 feet and the surrounding floor boards would be stained and polished.

On the appointed day a removal van and crew would turn up early in the morning and the entire contents of your house would be packed, transported and delivered to your new one. The last thing to be packed would be a teapot and mugs or cups so that the removal men could have a much-needed drink. These were the first things to be unpacked on arrival, ready for the next cuppa.

I never actually witnessed our next move which was to Wales. Mother, John and I would have stayed with Granny and Grandad at no. 16 next door. Father would have gone ahead of us and supervised everything down to the last detail.

Photo 8

Photo 9

Photo 10

8 My mother and her beloved father, John Henry Whitworth.
9 Engagement of Evelyn Whitworth and Maynard Cook.
10 My parents' wedding day.

CHAPTER TWELVE

I think it was early in the summer of 1937 when we moved to Wales. Our new home was in West Cross in the district of Mumbles, about four miles along the coast from the centre of Swansea. The wonderful thing for me was that as soon as we arrived a group of children knocked on the door to ask if I could come out to play. Playing turned out to be a game of rounders on a piece of land opposite our house called The Triangle because of its shape. Joy of joys, I hit a home run and was then an acceptable newcomer. Only one of the girls, Marjorie, went to my school and unfortunately we were not in the same form. However, we became close friends.

I had my 13th birthday that summer and to my great delight was given a full-sized bicycle. This meant that I could join in the game of Bicycle Polo that was played on Moorside Road where we lived. It was a road that had practically no traffic on it and was ideal for the purpose. Having a bicycle also meant that I could go on expeditions under my own steam instead of being given a lift on someone's crossbar.

Then there was Bonfire Night. Tradition had it that we built an enormous bonfire on the Triangle. Tradition also had it that a gang from the neighbouring village of Norton would surge up the hill to attack us. They would be expelled by clods of earth or anything else we could lay our hands on, including fire-crackers, being hurled at them. Nobody was ever hurt and I never encountered any subsequent ill-feeling between the two warring sides.

Mother didn't like our house very much. The only place where the sun shone was through the pantry window which was the last place you wanted it. Not only that, the back garden sloped up away from the house and that made it rather dark. We weren't there long before we moved to a house around the corner, fortunately also with easy access to the Triangle.

It was halfway through the Summer Term when I was transferred from Chesterfield High School to Swansea High School. Oh, what a difference! Shortly after my arrival I was taken to my form room where a history lesson was in progress. I was allocated a seat and was soon told to take a turn at reading aloud from my text book. Unfortunately, it was Welsh history and I was unable to pronounce all the strange names of people and places correctly. The tall, gaunt, formidable-looking teacher encouraged the other children to laugh at me in a contemptuous sort of way. She continued to bully me from then on, until one day just before I left I faced up to her. She went bright red with fury and then backed off and never bullied me again.

Not all the teachers were unpleasant and one or two were good. The German mistress upset me until I sussed out the problem. I had already done a year of German but now had to start the first year again. My previous teacher had told me that I had an authentic-sounding German accent, a simple matter for me as at that time I was a born mimic. This new woman castigated me for having an "appalling" accent when she first heard me read aloud. It was some time before I realised that she came from North Germany whereas my first teacher came from the South and the Northerners considered themselves superior and mocked the Southern accent. I recall the French Mademoiselle as being a fluffy, soft and gentle soul and I particularly liked the fair-minded, no-nonsense woman who taught us geometry and trigonometry.

Normally we were given at least two and a half hours of homework every night but on Wednesdays we had a lighter load. This was because of a radio programme called "Band Wagon", starring a funny little man called Arthur Askey. I think the entire nation listened to this programme, even our teachers, and they had the good sense to know that we wouldn't dream of missing it. Whether they were lenient over the homework out of the goodness of their hearts or because they were afraid of a mass rebellion I don't know.

Games and gymnastics played a much smaller part at my new school and we were still playing rounders and netball during my first year. It wasn't until the second year that we were taught hockey and tennis came later still. The hockey pitch was at the top of Town Hill and we went part way by bus and then walked up a hill so steep that it had a handrail up the middle of it.

Although I had played hockey at my old school I never got the chance to play in Swansea. I still had to make the journey to the pitch with the rest but along with one or two other rejects I just had to stand and watch. Gym was another major disappointment. The gymnasium was not particularly well equipped and I was informed that we were not allowed to climb the ropes until we were in the fifth form, a couple of years hence for me.

The Headmistress was a strange woman to say the least. She was dumpy and had thin, greyish hair which looked unwashed. I'm sure it was perfectly clean really; it just didn't look it to me. She had a thing about hair: it had to be tied back unless it was very short. One pigtail was ok but two pigtails were not. One day in the Biology Lab the girl next to me was absorbed in what she was doing when she felt something touching her hair and she started to brush whatever it was away with her hand. To her horror she found that it was the Headmistress, who had crept up behind her back and, down on her knees, was actually tying her two thick blonde pigtails together with string.

She had another obsession: no girl should speak to a boy on her way to or from school, not even if it was her brother. This might be considered prudery if it were not for the fact that she had redesigned the traditional gym slip so that there were no longer pleats all around but a plain front panel which overlapped a back panel. This could mean that a sizeable part of one's legs might be visible if there was a strong wind and you were running down the hill to catch a bus. Fortunately, there was sufficient overlap of material to prevent a flash of the navy blue knickers that were part of a girl's school uniform.

Actually where I lived you had to catch a train not a bus. This was not the usual sort of train. It was the famous Mumbles Train, that was the world's first passenger railway service. It made its first journey around the coast from Swansea to the Mumbles in 1807 and was of course horse-drawn; steam engines followed in 1877. When I lived in West Cross the train looked rather like a double-decker tram and the line had been electrified since 1929. The train was so close to the hearts of the people of Mumbles that when the line was closed in 1960 the residents dressed in black and held a wake.

The hill down to the train held a particular hazard for us girls: we were scared of a dog. It would run out of its gateway, snarling and growling. This savage beast that struck such terror into our hearts was a small Pekinese. Being built so close to the ground it was a real threat to our ankles. Help was always at hand though. The boys would come stomping along like an avenging army and with menacing growls of their own would send it scuttling back into its garden. Funnily enough we never encountered the little brute at any other time of the day.

Before we went to Wales we were informed, probably by people who had never been there, that it is always raining in South Wales. Certainly there was a local saying, "If you can see Devon on the horizon it's going to rain; if you can't see Devon it's already raining". I don't think that there was more rain than I was accustomed to, but they say that in one's memories of youth the sun always shines so who knows? What I did find was that there were times when the rain beat down so hard that it seemed to rise up again like a mist to an unbelievable height. Our school uniform included navy blue coats and really waterproof macs which we hung up on pegs in the school cloakroom. We also had indoor shoes and gym shoes in a drawstring bag hanging from the pegs and there was a sort of cubbyhole space in which to put our outdoor shoes, so we never seemed to suffer much from damp or cold.

At the end of Moorside Road there was a lane leading up to Clyne Common, another place of happy memories. It was on the Common that I was once persuaded to try smoking a cigarette. Naturally I didn't inhale and after two or three puffs I dismissed it as boring. This was a great disappointment to the boy who had hoped for a more dramatic effect from his gift of a cigarette.

The Common was beautiful and we spent a lot of time playing there. It also holds a special place in my heart and mind. Late one afternoon I was there completely alone when suddenly all the ferns and bracken turned to gold as the sun went down. It was magical and the world stopped still. I was filled with wonderment and a sense of peace, just as I had been some years before in my hayfield. What power beauty has over one's whole being!

At the top of the lane to the Common was a big, rambling old house where Polly, one of my friends, lived and where seemingly endless games of Monopoly were played. Polly's older brother Billy contracted glandular fever when he was young and this had left him with what we now call "learning difficulties". I may be mistaken but I had the impression that his father had written him off and had never tried to have him educated.

Billy would often go down the lane to call in on my mother and he could be sure of a welcome. Once he gave her a present, a set of Bridge pencils. I don't know where he got them from, he couldn't have bought them as he was never given any money as far as I know. Mother didn't like playing any card games, let alone Bridge, but because his own mother spent most of her time sitting in her drawing room or playing Bridge, Billy thought that was what mothers did and so it was his way of expressing his feelings for my mother. Billy and I were also good friends. Somebody told me years later that Billy had been sent to the West Country during the War to work on the land. I hope that he was happy there.

On Sundays we trotted off to the church hall in Blackpill, another little district, further down the coast in the opposite direction from Norton, the village of Bonfire Night fame. There we were taught all that was needed for us to be confirmed by the Bishop. I don't think that any of us were particularly religious, going to Sunday school was just accepted as the normal thing to do.

A rather elderly little lady twittered away at us and we sinners tormented her by asking questions such as, "Please, what is adultery?" Once a week the sessions took place in our lovely little church and were conducted by the Vicar. He was young and good-looking and had a wonderful voice. When he preached, you listened, not necessarily taking in what he said, just for the joy of hearing him. My friends were in the choir and they asked the Vicar if I might sit with them. Bless the man, he said, "Yes, she can but not to sing!" I think the Welsh thought they had the sole rights to choral music – or maybe he had once heard me carolling away to myself and didn't wish to repeat the experience.

The large village of Mumbles lay to the west, just beyond Norton. Its centre was Oystermouth which boasted a castle fairly high up on a mound with beautiful views of Swansea Bay to the west and along the coast westward to the pier and the lighthouse. I read with interest not long ago that Wales has more castles than any other country in the world.

The pier was at the tip of the bay and as you rounded the bend towards all the beautiful bays of the Gower coast there before you was the lighthouse. The pier was never used for shipping, it was purely for pleasure and amusements and you could spend your pocket money getting your innards jolted and your bones broken on the dodgem cars.

There was also a cinema where we saw the likes of Mickey Rooney, Judy Garland and Deanna Durbin – she of the beautiful voice. These films were passed by the censor for general viewing but on one occasion we wanted to see one that required an accompanying adult. No problem, we made up a fifteen strong party and the oldest boy asked for "one and fourteen halves please" and we were in.

It was a pity that we changed house yet again and that period of my childhood ended. But we were all getting older and moving on anyway, nothing lasts for ever.

CHAPTER THIRTEEN

Once again I do not know, or perhaps just don't remember, why we moved. Our new home was a lovely bungalow between the bays of Langland and Caswell. It was up a winding driveway and invisible from the main road which led down to Caswell Bay. It was of an unusual design; the front door was round the back so we always used the kitchen entrance where there was a delightful little garden in which we grew some sweet-smelling plants, such as mignonette, a favourite of Mother's, as well as a few herbs, lettuces, radishes, etc.

The front or rear door was of glass and next to it was a large window overlooking the back garden. The glazed door led into a room, or large hall, which we used as a dining room. To one side of this was a bedroom and on the other side the lounge. To the rear was a hallway leading to two more bedrooms and the bathroom and kitchen. The garden was one huge expanse of grass backing onto part of the golf course and beyond that was the sea.

My mother loved that bungalow; I think we all did. I know that John was happy there; not only did he have a good circle of friends but his asthma was no longer so troublesome, possibly because he spent so much of his time out on the sea, paddling a canoe with his closest friend, John Moriarty. I remember they used to take the portable wind-up gramophone with them and strains of the latest songs could be faintly heard if the wind was in the right direction. That gramophone was much travelled. Mother used to take it to Bournemouth with her on her earlier visits. It was also remarkably resilient as it survived a ducking when one day the canoe capsized; I don't know which of the boys dived to rescue it from a watery grave.

In 1954 I took the same gramophone to Canada with me and it was still going strong in 1957 when I gave it to a friend's children to keep them amused during their long journey from the west to the east of the country. If it is still in existence it will be over 90 years old. These machines can sometimes be seen in antique shows on the television.

We now lived about six miles from Swansea and there was nobody of my age living in the neighbourhood so my only real friend was Marjorie who lived in West Cross. We walked back and forth to each other's homes using the short cut through the cemetery or met up in Oystermouth. The journey to school was now longer and involved a bus as well as the train.

However, I still managed to get home for lunch. I don't suppose the mad rush to achieve this was any more harmful to my digestive system than eating school dinners would have been. After school, I would very occasionally walk all the way home just for the pleasure of it. I was now fourteen and for the next two or three years found walking an antidote to the low moods that can sometimes bedevil teenagers, not that "teenagers" had been invented then.

It was about this time that Mother was told a strange story by Mrs Moriarty, the Irish mother of John's canoeing friend. A Gypsy woman turned up at her kitchen door one day and she gave her a cup of tea, in return for which the Gypsy offered to tell her fortune. At that time she had just one child and was not anticipating having another but the Gypsy told her that she would have another son and predicted exactly when he would be born, some ten years in the future. She also said that her first son would die in an aeroplane when he was seventeen. As the fortune telling took place in the 1920's when there was no thought of war, her son's death in an aeroplane seemed unlikely. But when to her surprise she did produce another son at the time predicted the coincidence was a little alarming.

At the outbreak of war in 1939 the older boy joined the RAF and was sent to Canada for training as a pilot. He died in a flying accident; he was seventeen years old. We had left Swansea by the time this happened but my brother, who was also in the RAF and training in Canada, told us what had happened. Mother was not a believer in the supernatural or

106

fortune telling and probably thought it was coincidental. For my part, common sense told me to agree with her, but all the same I didn't want anyone to predict what my future might hold.

Langland Bay was only a short walk away, down what I remember as more of a lane than a road or you could take a short cut skirting the golf course. I was not so keen on the golf course route. I half expected to be hit on the back of my head by a golf ball. Always the back of my head I suppose because otherwise I might see the ball coming and be able to take evasive action.

We had a green canvas beach hut at the golf course end of the Bay and spent every Sunday and some other days as well loafing by the sea. My fear of putting my head under water had remained with me and I still couldn't swim. I would happily splash around and walk into the sea until the water came up to my chin. One day I inadvertently stepped down into deep water and found that I could swim after all. As it was a case of sink or swim, I swam. Life at the Bay became ever more enjoyable.

On Sunday 3rd September 1939, just before setting out for our usual day at the beach, we switched on the wireless to hear Prime Minister Neville Chamberlain's address to the nation. He informed us that we were now at war with Germany.

This news came as no great surprise as we had been anticipating the possibility for the past year. In spite of Chamberlain's appeasement policies and his visits to Munich and meeting with Adolf Hitler it was a vain hope that Hitler could be deterred from continuing his rampage of conquest over Europe. On Chamberlain's return from his final visit to Germany he declared that he had brought "peace for our time". He may have believed it but many people thought it unlikely. There were no grounds for hoping that words of sweet reason would stop a madman like Hitler from invading the rest of Europe.

Hitler had annexed Austria in 1938 and in March 1939 had occupied all of Czechoslovakia. Next on his list was Poland, with whom France and Britain had made an agreement of mutual support. Therefore when Germany invaded Poland on 1st September 1939 Chamberlain was forced to honour the agreement and war was declared two days later.

Nobody anticipated that the War would last for six long years; indeed there were those that said it would be "all over by Christmas". Wishful thinking gone berserk! What we had not known was just how unprepared for war our country was. The fighting spirit was there in abundance but the necessary arms and equipment were all in short supply. A policy of appeasement is all very well but you have to draw the line somewhere and that line had now been drawn.

Swansea had its share of bombing and destruction but we were not there to witness it. Once more we had moved and were now living in the historic and lovely old city of Chester.

CHAPTER FOURTEEN

In late 1939 Father found a new place of work in the City of Chester. Mother, John and I remained in our bungalow between the Bays of Langland and Caswell for a further two or three weeks while he was settling in and looking for a new home for us.

The winter of 1939/40 was bitterly cold with more snow than Swansea had experienced for many years; indeed, it was so cold that the sea froze, which was almost unheard of. Our leather-soled shoes made walking hazardous and people were resorting to encasing them in old socks or rags to prevent slipping. This helped a little but the socks soon wore away. It was during this period that Father contracted measles whilst working in Chester and, with hindsight, I'm pretty sure it permanently undermined his health and strength.

I don't know whether it was the icy weather or a reluctance on Mother's part to leave a home she was happy in that delayed our departure from Swansea, but eventually Father returned and organised our move to Chester. He had found us a lovely old two-storey house which we rented from a small elderly lady who lived in the adjoining house with her rather malevolent black cat. She was as tough as old boots and a quite formidable character.

Our new house was just under two miles to the west of the city centre in an enclave called Upton Park, a turning off the main road leading to the village of Upton. At the entrance to this was an old mill, into which an aeroplane had crashed and become embedded. After about a hundred yards, the road divided and formed a circle at the far end of which was another exit. All the houses were old and some of them had large gardens with lots of trees running parallel with the roadway so that you almost had a sense of being in a country lane. The surface of the road had quite a few potholes, which got deeper as time went by and could be rather a hazard when cycling home in the black-out. Cars presented no problem as apart from the fact that Upton Park would not have been used as a through road to anywhere there were not many of them about; petrol was in short supply and rationed and only those with a real need seemed to have enough petrol coupons to drive anywhere.

Upton Park had the feel of a close community in spite of the houses being large and not close together. One lady who was divorced, very elegant and tended to keep herself to herself drove a pony and trap and she would stop and give Mother a lift in it from time to time. Then there was Mrs Anderson, a buxom lady with prominent teeth who never seemed to stop speaking if you walked along the road with her from the bus stop. She lived next door to Peggy, with whom my brother had struck up a relationship. Peggy's father and John got on very well together but John was not so enthusiastic about her mother. This liaison didn't last all that long for two reasons. John was posted to Canada and Mother, who was extremely possessive of her son, was determined to freeze Peggy out. I tended to be on Mother's side for once. Like most of the women in the Park I thought Peggy was a little gold digger and certainly nobody liked their husbands to be on fire watching duty with her. Some twenty or so years later when I met up with John in Canada and we were reminiscing I mentioned the gold digger label the worthy women of Upton Park had slapped on Peggy. He grinned and said with some satisfaction, "Oh, sure, but she gave good value for money."

At the far end of the Park lived the three Sabine girls. They had a smooth-haired, bad-tempered dog aptly named Nipper that I remember being scared of. The youngest girl was quite attractive; I cannot recall the middle one and the oldest was built like an Amazon. John once described her rather unkindly as having a shelf in front and a shelf behind. They were all three stalwart members of the fire watching group.

Then there were the Miss Dames, two tall elderly ladies dressed in long lavender-coloured dresses and straw hats, often glimpsed with gardening trugs and secateurs, looking as though they had been left over from the 19th century. They were looked after by an equally elderly housekeeper. It seemed that they approved of Mother because they would give her apples from their garden; there was one lovely old cooking apple which gloried in the name "Peasgood's Nonsuch".

On the other side of the road, opposite their big three-storey house lived Tom Williams and his wife and later their twin baby boys. Tom was a redhead and in the Merchant Navy. He was of a carefree disposition and he and Father got on very well together. Tom occasionally managed to get hold of a bottle of rum and he would give it to Father so that he could have a tot now and again to help him sleep, something which the doctor had recommended but had failed to supply.

When Tom was badly injured and then sent home to recuperate he was confined to a downstairs bedroom. As there was a large hedge in front of their house and garden we all considered that he had complete privacy. Not so, the Miss Dames complained that he could be seen in a state of undress; shock, horror! But joy of joys we all realised that there was only one small top landing window high up on the side of their house from which there was the slightest possibility of seeing into Tom's bedroom. You can imagine the glee that their complaint was greeted with.

Next to the Mill in which the aeroplane had become embedded was Mill House. This was inhabited by Brenda, an extremely attractive young woman who was married to an Air Force officer stationed abroad somewhere. Brenda had a mother and a sister who sometimes visited her; the three of them were so incredibly alike they could have been triplets. At one time they had been on the stage as a triple act, I think at the Windmill Theatre in London, and now the mother was the Wardrobe Mistress there. Brenda had a succession of Canadian officers billeted upon her and was the soul of kindness and friendliness to all and sundry. It was noticeable that not a single wife or mother in the vicinity had anything but a good word to say about her.

Brenda was of a practical nature and could tackle anything. Mother and Father were away from home for a day or two and I was alone apart from the couple who were billeted on us. A box arrived by post and to my horror on opening it I found a dead chicken with head and feathers still intact that some kind person had sent as a gift to my parents. There was no way I could deal with this; I had and still have a horror of dead birds, or dead animals come to that. I went down the road to see Brenda. "Give it to me," she said. "I'll draw it and pluck it for you."

If you continue up the main road at the beginning of Upton Park you come to Chester Zoo at Upton. During the war many animals were evacuated from London to this wonderful zoo. I had never liked the idea of animals being in captivity, so it was with some reluctance that I agreed to visit the zoo with a friend. I was so impressed by it; one of the things I remember is an island on which all the monkeys were playing happily among trees. Now that there has been a series on television about the formation and life of the zoo there is no point in my trying to recall it and set down a description. What was of interest to me was that Tom Williams, when he was more or less recovered from his injuries went to work there for a while. I was told that he then became rather too friendly with one of the lions and suffered a bit of a mauling.

Father told us that our house was 135 years old so it must have been built in 1805 in the reign of George III. Although it was old it didn't show any sign of deterioration and it was of beautiful proportions. Both the dining-room and the drawing-room looked out onto the large lawned front garden, which was sheltered from the road by shrubs and an old walnut tree. Mother pickled the walnuts when she could collect enough of them before any marauding children sneaked in and pinched them, thinking they were horse chestnuts.

A long driveway led past the entrance porch at the side of the house to an outbuilding which presumably had once housed a horse-drawn vehicle. A coal store and outside lavatory had been added on at a later date; I assume that the coal would have been kept in one of the cellars previously. Both the kitchen and the breakfast room faced the back garden which was separated from the adjacent field by a line of pear trees, all of which were so old that they no longer produced much in the way of edible fruit.

Upstairs were three double and one single bedroom; a fifth bedroom had been made into a bathroom and over the porch was a small room containing a lavatory and washbasin and enough space for a large chest of drawers. It was a complete change from our bungalow in Wales and I daresay Mother felt somewhat daunted by its size but fortunately she liked it very much, as did the rest of us.

It was as well that the house was large because it wasn't long before my grandparents came to live with us. Grandad Whitworth had suffered a minor nervous breakdown and been forced to retire. We had quite a problem preventing him from going out into the garden during air raids to "see what's happening". I remember poor Granny sitting on the cellar steps nursing a broken wrist and worrying about him. Subsequently, they returned home to Chesterfield, let out their house in Tennyson Avenue and rented one in Dronfield, a small town between Chesterfield and Sheffield.

We were not on our own for long as accommodation was needed for the influx of war workers and members of the Forces. Two of our rooms were taken by a married couple with whom we shared the bathroom and kitchen. They had the use of the back garden and we had the front.

The husband was not a good-looking man in the accepted sense of the word but friendliness and good humour shone in his face. Mother described him as having "a nice type of ugliness", a phrase which she had used about a friend of my brother's in Swansea. I couldn't have agreed with her more as I well remember the boy in question; he was the only one of John's friends who deigned to acknowledge my existence and I could easily have fallen in love him at the age of fifteen. Alas, he was one of the first to lose his life in the War.

The wife – I can't remember their names – was the only woman we knew who could carry off what was the current fashion of wearing her coat draped over her shoulders with the sleeves hanging loose without it falling off or restricting her movements. She would come home from work, sail into the kitchen and start preparing a meal without taking off her coat or putting on an apron. In fact I don't think she even possessed an apron. Mother regaled me with the story of how she saw her frying an egg one day and dropping it on the floor. Nothing daunted, she scooped it up and popped it on the plate. When you consider that our egg ration at that time was only one egg per person per week you can understand why. After all, her husband would never have known what happened to it and probably wouldn't have worried if he had.

CHAPTER FIFTEEN

Chester survived the War relatively unscathed; it was not a target of the German bombers in spite of the fact that it contained the Headquarters of Western Command and that there were many Army camps in the vicinity. It was, however, on a direct route to Liverpool so we had frequent air raid warnings. Sometimes the Germans would jettison their bombs around Chester if our defences had prevented them from getting into Liverpool. We had not been there very long before a bomb landed in our neighbouring field but at that very early stage of the War bombs were not very large and we were not affected by it although it did make quite a big crater. What we did have though was a plane crashing into and becoming embedded in the Mill at the corner of Upton Park and the main road.

Father had joined the newly-formed Local Defence Volunteers, which was to be renamed the Home Guard, but as his health deteriorated he had to give that up. He did, however, organise our local fire watchers for as long as he was able and this must have required no small amount of tact and man-management. There were some male residents who wanted to be on duty with one or two of the women but were reluctant to be out alone in the blackout with two or three of the others, particularly the one who was built like a young Amazon – they joked among themselves that they feared for their virtue! Everybody was issued with a gas mask but fortunately we never had to make use of them. We also had a stirrup pump which was to be used in conjunction with buckets of water to put out fires. I don't know how effective it would have been because we were lucky enough to have no need of it. John and I tried it out as a window cleaning device but it wasn't a huge success and we ended up dousing each other with it instead.

The school leaving age in 1940 was 14 but if you attended a Grammar or High School it was 16, by which time you would have taken the Lower School Certificate examination. If you were bright enough you stayed at school until you were 18 when, hopefully, you gained your Higher School Certificate. The curriculum in Wales was rather different to the English one; there you studied for the Central Welsh Board examination which was roughly equivalent to the Lower School Cert.

I had not enjoyed the change of school from Chesterfield to Swansea and as by now I had missed one whole term of schooling I would once again be at a disadvantage were I to start another new school halfway through the Spring term. It was highly unlikely that I could pass the Lower School Certificate exam in the summer. To my great relief it was decided that I should help with the household chores and the gardening and explore the city of Chester with Mother until I was a little older.

Chester was a surprise to me. I had not known anything about it except that it had been built as a fortress by the Romans in the first century AD. The four main streets in the city were fascinating as they were lined with two-tiered galleried arcades of shops, called The Rows. These were mainly half-timbered and Tudor looking, although some are reputed to be 700 years old. Eastgate is particularly attractive with a large clock surmounting the bridge that crosses the street. The city wall encircles the central part of the town and passes close to the magnificent cathedral. In addition to Eastgate, there are Watergate, Northgate and Foregate Streets and Bridge Street, which leads down to the River Dee. You can walk all the way around the City wall; it takes quite a long time as I am told it is about two miles in length.

In early 1940 there seemed to be no shortage of food and one of my abiding memories is of a café and restaurant called "Quaintways" with its comfortable seating reminiscent of the café in Sheffield that I went to as a child with Mother and Granny Whitworth. The problem was what to choose; all the cakes were so tempting. Lots of fresh cream cakes and meringues that were of just the right consistency. There was an apple confection, too, that I was particularly fond of. Very soon all this changed and food rationing altered our eating habits for many years to come. It was not until 1954 that all rationing ended.

Quaintways later became the venue for Saturday night dancing in the upstairs ballroom. It was all very respectable; parents didn't have cause to worry, at any rate not until everybody wended their way home or back to camp. Nobody would have been allowed entry if they had been drinking too much or looked as though they might cause trouble. Dancing and socialising with the opposite sex was what it was all about with hopes of a new romance thrown in for good measure.

The shops in the Rows and at ground level were well stocked with goods which appeared to be of a better quality than those in Swansea. Cheshire was a wealthier area than South Wales and of course Chester was the county town so it was only natural that there would be a greater demand for the more expensive merchandise. One day when Mother and I were exploring we found, tucked away in the Rows, a small shop specialising in crumpets and pikelets. I daresay it went out of business when butter was severely rationed – a crumpet is not a crumpet if it doesn't drip butter down your fingers.

Another surprise find was in Watergate Street. Suddenly a door opened and an enormous cheese was rolled out. We had always enjoyed cheese and Cheshire was one of our favourites, but we had never before tasted any to compare with that which we ate in Chester. Of course it was nothing like the square lumps of the stuff sold shrink-wrapped in the supermarkets of today. To see it rolled out like a great big lorry wheel straight from the cheese factors was what made it extra special and I have never forgotten it.

Writing about these early days of the war seems a little unreal. They didn't last for very long and the period was later referred to as "the Phoney War". There may have been many other parts of the country that didn't fare so well but I can only record my own experiences.

In 1940 the War was not going well for us and Neville Chamberlain was not an effective wartime leader. In May, the German army had surged through the Ardennes with tanks and destroyed the port of Rotterdam and the Dutch surrendered and when by mid-May our British Expeditionary Force was surrounded they were also forced to surrender.

This was the start of our withdrawal and escape from Dunkirk, a port in northern France. Although it was undoubtedly a defeat it has always been hailed by us as a sort of victory with the navy evacuating nearly 400,000 of our troops with the assistance of a vast number of small privately owned boats. Anybody who had a boat of any sort, large or small, sailed across the Channel to help bring our soldiers back. Our neighbour Tom Williams was involved in this rescue operation. Whether or not it is true I don't know but the story was that having had the front of their vessel holed they made the return journey by sailing in reverse. Unfortunately all our tanks and equipment fell into German hands and in June the Belgians capitulated and we were on our own and facing invasion.

By now we had Winston Churchill as our Prime Minister, Neville Chamberlain having resigned. Churchill had been a war correspondent in the Boer War and had fought in France in the First World War. He was a great orator and his speeches and the way in which he delivered them stiffened everyone's backbone and gave them hope. One remembers him declaring that "...we shall fight on the beaches, we shall fight on the landing grounds, we shall fight in the fields and in the streets, we shall fight in the hills; we shall never surrender..." All stirring stuff!

In June 1940 when France was on the verge of defeat their Prime Minister, Petain, signed an armistice with Hitler, which allowed a third of France to remain unoccupied. Petain was considered to be a collaborator and a traitor but was spared the death sentence at the end of the war and was imprisoned for life instead. The French General de Gaulle escaped to England and from there organised the Free French as a fighting force. Also in Britain were the squadrons of Polish and Czech airmen who fought so gallantly alongside us in The Battle of Britain that summer.

By October, having failed in spite of the devastation caused by his relentless bombing of London and other cities, to defeat us and force us to give up, Hitler abandoned his plans for invasion. It was a good job for us that he did; we were really not well enough equipped to have successfully resisted him.

It was in 1941 that women were mobilised for the first time ever and sent to join the ATS, WRNS or the WAAF. These were the female equivalent of the Army, Navy and Air Force. Some women joined the Land Army to grow and harvest the food we needed; others were directed to work in the factories and to do many of the jobs previously done by men. Mother was eventually called up for interview but was never conscripted, possibly because she had a son in the Air Force, me in a reserved occupation, two war workers living in her house and a husband who was not in the best of health.

It seems that in some circumstances age is no barrier to being in uniform. One day I was amazed to see an elderly lady, resplendent in ATS uniform, riding a bicycle along Northgate Street. I was later to learn that she was 74 years old and a long-serving member from the First World War and a special case. I was also told that she was well-known and respected for work which she had done on some of the magnificent carvings in Chester Cathedral.

We had not been self-sufficient as regards food before the War and now we had to remedy that. We could not just depend on imports from America that our Merchant Navy was heroically crossing the

Atlantic to bring to us. They were escorted there and back by our warships but still suffered heavy losses from the German U-boat attacks. People grew vegetables in their gardens, allotments or any spare bits of vacant land; naturally the more exotic fruits like bananas, oranges and other citrus fruits disappeared until after the War. It has been said since that our diet was far healthier than it is today and I can well believe it. We ate hardly any sugar, sweets or chocolate but lots of vegetables and all the fruits native to this country.

Franklin Roosevelt, the American President, had been elected for a third term of office, to some extent on the grounds that he promised that no Americans would be killed in war. Thinking that it would be more likely that this promise could be kept if he supported us, he introduced a Lease Lend Scheme, whereby he could send us armaments, machinery, etc. When Japan entered the war he foresaw that hostilities with them were inevitable and he introduced conscription in the US for the first time ever. In December 1941 Japan bombed Pearl Harbour and America entered the war.

The arrival of American GIs into Britain was not greeted with unbridled enthusiasm by our menfolk as they seemed able to conjure up an endless supply of nylon stockings, lipsticks and Hershey Bars, with which to attempt the seduction of our girls and they made the most of these advantages. This gave rise to the well-known complaint that they were "over-paid, over-sexed and over here". Criticising the Americans was perhaps a little unfair as they were only behaving in exactly the same way that any army behaves when a long way from home. Their girlfriends came in for a spot of criticism, too; they were sometimes thought of as being 'of easy virtue'. I don't recall ever meeting an American soldier, let alone going out with one, so I am in no position to make judgements; maybe there weren't any stationed around Chester.

Nowadays it is difficult if not impossible to understand how on earth people managed to make good, filling and appetising meals when food was rationed not only during wartime but for so long afterwards. Mother was gifted in this task, possibly helped by her natural charm and good looks. For example, the butcher in Chester Market was a good source of supply of offal which although not rationed was naturally in short supply. In addition to our meat ration, we were allotted two pennyworth of corned beef per person per week. If we saved our twopennyworth up for a month we could get a tin of it, from which Mother would make a delicious corned beef loaf.

Any fatty bits of meat which Mother had wangled from the butcher she would render down in order to eke out the fat ration and make pastry or a cake. Although for much of the time we only had one egg a week we could get tins of dried egg, probably from America, and this made quite palatable scrambled egg on toast. Our milk was delivered by horse and cart. Both the horse and the milkman appeared to be of great age and due to their extremely slow gait were locally known as "Lightning". Mr Lightning was a lovely man and later on when Father was not well he would occasionally find an extra egg to give to him. Doing this seemed to give him as much pleasure as it gave Mother to receive it.

CHAPTER SIXTEEN

The one drawback of not going to school was the lack of companionship with my own age group. However, I did meet Betty Pomeroy who lived with her brother and his wife at the corner of Upton Park opposite the Mill. She had been lucky enough to have left Guernsey in the nick of time when it fell into German hands. The brother was a pilot in the Air Transport Auxiliary and intended to start an air transport line of his own when the war ended.

Betty must have been a little older than I was because she had a job in a shop as a book-keeper or cashier. She sat in a cage in the upper regions and received the money and bills that were despatched from the counters to run along the overhead wires for her to deal with. She wasn't altogether happy living with her brother as she couldn't come to terms with their lifestyle of strip-poker games and what had become his too close relationship with one of his wife's friends who was also living with them. This affair ultimately led to divorce and Betty left Chester.

It was about this time that I made the train journey from Chester back to Swansea to visit my old school-friend Marjorie. The train was a slow one, travelling south through the middle of Wales and it was an evening journey. All the names of the stations had been removed to ensure that any enemy entering Britain would have no idea where they were. This was particularly inconvenient after nightfall as there were of course no lights because of the blackout so there were times when we British might well not have known where we were either. I do remember that at that time Swansea had two railway stations and that I arrived at the wrong one about midnight, just as the air raid sirens were starting to wail.

Unlike Chester, Swansea had suffered rather badly from the bombing that had started in the autumn of 1940. From Marjorie's house in West Cross you could see right over to Town Hill where her grandparents lived. The Germans had fire-bombed Swansea and Marjorie told me of how she and her family had stood watching one night when Town Hill was ablaze and how helpless and fearful they had felt. Her grandparents were among the lucky ones who survived but many must have lost their homes if not their lives.

Now it so happened that during my visit I developed a pretty heavy cold, not a pleasant experience for me or my hosts. But it was on this holiday that I discovered a dramatic and what some might today call a traumatic cold cure. Marjorie and I decided to go to a bay that we had been to several times in the past; it was called Pwildu and you reached it by walking through Bishopston Valley. All the bays on the Gower Coast have their own individual charm and on this occasion we were so charmed that we left it rather late before starting our homeward journey and darkness fell before we had expected it to.

We entered the valley and it was just a little scary finding our way but we were not too bothered. Then suddenly, out of the darkness, strange, threatening shapes kept appearing and disappearing, some of which seemed to be coming to attack us. We were terrified and we started to run and we ran and ran, faster and faster, and still they came. We were both sweating with fear and exhaustion by the time we reached the roadway.

From that moment my cold disappeared and not even a sniffle was left. We did feel a little stupid, though, when we found out later that the monsters looming up out of the dark were cows!

On my return from Swansea, Father said, "I think it would be a good idea for you to go to secretarial school now; you've done enough loafing about." I agreed wholeheartedly and was duly enrolled at a small secretarial establishment run by Miss Mann. She was well named; she wore grey suits with a white shirt blouse and a necktie and taught us shorthand and book-keeping. Her partner in this enterprise was a very feminine and gentle soul who taught typing. It was only on looking back years later that I realised that in all probability they were partners in life as well as in business.

I enjoyed learning shorthand and typing but felt that book-keeping was not for me. I explained to Miss Mann that I neither liked nor was I very good at it so it might be a good idea to drop the subject. She said, "That would be a pity, it might be a requirement when you apply for a job." I replied that I wouldn't apply for any job that needed book-keeping. "Well," she said, "You had better discuss the matter with your father." So I did and, as I knew he would, he reckoned that to continue learning book-keeping would be a waste of both Miss Mann's time and mine.

The course was supposed to last for six months but at the end of four months Miss Mann asked me and a girl called Gill if we would consider taking a job as she had received a request for two shorthand typists. Apparently she considered us to be her two most qualified pupils so off we went to work for what I think was called The Sweet, Chocolate and Cake Manufacturing Association. Gill seemed reasonably happy there but I disliked it intensely. It was not a friendly atmosphere. I hated both my typewriter, which I think was called an L.C. Smith, and the work involved.

The top brass of the member companies regularly visited Chester for meetings and one of my duties was to set up the Boardroom for the well-dressed and, to my mind, rather self-important people who descended on us. I suppose I was prejudiced because rationing was beginning to bite and I rather resented these men lunching on lobster patties, rich desserts and other such goodies as though it were everyday fare for all and sundry. Ever the socialist at heart, I thought they could at least look appreciative of what we provided them with. I remember one man arriving with a huge tin containing a Terry's Rich Fruit Cake, which they managed to scoff in no time flat, all perks of the job of course. It was not sour grapes on my part as I couldn't stand fruit cake and was not particularly impressed by lobster patties.

Then one glorious day Miss Mann telephoned me to say that she had a feeling that I wasn't altogether happy or settling in at my job. It did cross my mind that my employers might not like me any more than I liked them but she was kind enough not to say so. Anyway, it transpired that Western Command had need of a shorthand typist and Miss Mann thought that I might like to go for an interview. "Might like?" I jumped at the chance and made my way to Oak House on the other side of the River Dee that very evening.

Oak House and its next door neighbour Fern House had been requisitioned by the Army to house the Royal Army Ordnance Corps' office staff and although by the time I arrived there most of the staff had already gone home there was an atmosphere of warmth and friendliness about the place. I was met by the head of the typing pool and a Senior Warrant Officer who was apparently the Chief Clerk and given a rather perfunctory test of my skills. I must have given a good account of myself or else they were desperate for an additional typist as I was hired on the spot and went home in a state of euphoria.

Both Oak House and Fern House had been quite large family homes and I think that this is what gave everybody who worked in them a sense of belonging. There certainly was not the impersonal atmosphere of purpose built offices.

I was shown into a large downstairs room and presented with an ancient Brothers portable typewriter and a load of things to type up. I soon learnt that nobody had expected me to be able to achieve anything and were stunned into admiration when I managed to beat the old, nearly defunct Brothers machine back into life.

Two old civilian men were in charge of this office and in normal circumstances they would have been retired; one was 63 and I think the other was a year older. Men of that age are not considered old today but 75 years ago they were, and certainly these two were a bit doddery. The word was, though, that you needed to watch out if you found yourself working alone with one of them on a Sunday morning when only a skeleton staff would be on duty.

Our section dealt with vehicles and we were responsible for equipping units with what they needed, which meant we sent out the paperwork and authority to shift vehicles all over the country. Two of the girls had worked there from the start of hostilities and told the story of how, in spite of a complete lack of experience, they had been charged with the task of requisitioning motor vehicles during the first few months. A tricky business as they weren't at all sure what, if any, compensation should be given to their owners. All those stories that one has heard about us not being fully prepared for war and probably having to beat off an invading army with pitchforks had a certain ring of truth about them.

Eventually someone procured a full-sized typewriter for me, which was quite an achievement as everything was in short supply. We also had a reshuffle of rooms because I remember it being lighter and brighter than when I started work there and the two old men were no longer in evidence. There were two young Army officers from whom I took dictation, one of them had a speech impediment and got stuck on the letter "L". He would ring for Dot Brown, one of the clerks, and ask her to bring him the Location Statement and there were times when she had time to fetch it for him before he had managed to get further than "Llll …" He was not hurt or offended by this largely because they were rather more than good friends and I think they married after the war ended.

We were a mixed bunch of civilian and Army personnel. Women were not conscripted into the forces until 1941 and those of us who had already started working there or were still under the age of conscription were considered to be in a "reserved occupation" and not liable to be drafted into the Services nor could we resign. The first member of the ATS (the women's branch of the Army) that I worked with was about 30 and was only with our branch for a short time. She was Jewish and a daughter of the family which founded the Berkatrex fashion house. I have tried and failed to remember her surname, which was very similar, a bit like Battenberg being changed to Mountbatten. She was fun and interesting and confessed to having a strong liking for bacon, which she found almost impossible to resist. A good job it was rationed, it saved her from sinning more often.

Her place was taken by a young woman who suffered from epilepsy. This scared the living daylights out of me. Sorry as I was for her, I was selfishly more concerned for myself as I would not have known how to deal with the situation if we were on duty together and she had a fit. She, too, was posted elsewhere before long.

All the senior staff were Army officers, Captains or Majors, with non-commissioned officers supervising the work of their particular sections. The Registry for example was run by a Staff Sergeant. I remember him because he was a nice, youngish man with a nearly bald head over which he combed a few strands of long hair. It says a lot for his personality that it never made him look silly.

The Chief Clerk, who I had met at my interview for the job, was in overall charge of all clerical and typing staff, civilian or Army, and seemed to be responsible for the smooth running of the whole place. I came to know him reasonably well and he once invited me home to meet his wife and baby daughter. It had been suggested to him several times that he should apply for a commission but he resolutely turned the idea down. As a Warrant Officer 1 he was well paid but as a 2nd Lieutenant he would have had too much additional expenditure and be at the bottom of the pile, so to speak, whereas he was now at the top of his pile.

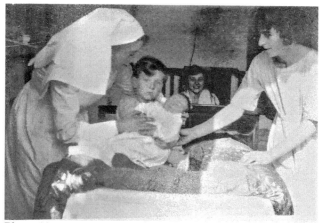

Photo 11

Photo 12   Photo 13

11 Brother John meeting his new baby sister.
12 My first formal photograph.
13 Roger, the Airedale, joins the ice-cream party.

Photo 14

Photo 15

Photo 16

Photo 17

14 Father enjoying time with his children.
15 John wearing his new school uniform.
16 The Cook family in Tennyson Avenue, Chesterfield.
17 John and Sara-Louise's wedding day.

CHAPTER SEVENTEEN

One of the advantages of working for Western Command was that you could lunch in the NAAFI canteen if you didn't wish to bring sandwiches from home. There was no need to hand over any coupons or points from your ration book for this privilege as you were sometimes required to do if you were dining out in restaurants, depending on what you had selected from the menu. On the other hand, NAAFI food was not always that appetising; sausages were something that I learnt to check on before purchasing to make sure they were well cooked. But on the whole it was excellent value and you ate in good company.

On one occasion I found that it was not only the state of the sausages that you had to look out for. I went to the canteen counter for a cup of tea and then rejoined my friends. I picked up my cup and was about to take a first sip when I noticed something floating in the tea. It looked remarkably like a small piece of bread. I stirred it and lo and behold there was another, this time unidentified, tiny lump of something. Back I trotted to the counter and laughingly showed it to the girl saying, "This looks more like washing-up water than tea!" She peered at it and in horror cried, "Oh my God, it is; they've filled it from the slops urn!" I don't know how many customers had started drinking their tea before looking into the cup.

The NAAFI was also where dances were sometimes held. To this day I remember a young Welsh subaltern whirling me around the floor in an old fashioned waltz. It was remarkable because I wasn't much of a ballroom dancer and certainly not by any reckoning even a halfway good exponent of the old-fashioned waltz, but there I was flying around the room and never putting a foot wrong. It was sheer bliss and never to be repeated.

By now it was the winter of 1941/42 and I had settled in well in my new job. Everyone was very friendly. One of my friends – called, I think, Beryl, but I remember her as "Beb" – decided that I was perhaps a little too frivolous and empty-headed and sought to make me into a more serious-minded individual. She took me off to the Toc H to sort through their large chest of books of the more serious kind. Toc H had been founded in the 1st World War as an inter-denominational Christian fellowship by the Reverend P.T.B. Clayton, commonly known as "Tubby" Clayton. The building was named Talbot House but became "Toc H" from the Army signallers' designation of its initials. There was at one time a saying that something or someone was "as dim as a Toc H lamp" so I can only assume that either the lighting was poor in the original chapel or club or that it referred to a lamp hanging outside the building.

I went there with Beb in a bid to improve my mind, only to find that I had already read most of the books, including "War and Peace". Beb must have been into Russian authors at the time as she suggested "Crime and Punishment" by Dostoievski which I had also read. I forget what we settled for in the end.

When the summer weather came, Beb decided I should join her on a youth hostelling expedition and this I did a couple of times. I think we went by train into North Wales, which is of course so near to Chester. Indeed it was near enough for there to be a saying, just like the one about Devon and Swansea, this was "If you can see Moel Famau from here, it is going to rain; if you can't see Moel Famau from here, it is already raining." Moel is Welsh for mountain, so its height would have made it visible.

Youth hostelling was a revelation to me as I had never heard anything at all about it. When we arrived I found that we would be sleeping in a dormitory with three-tier bunks and that we had to perform a quota of domestic chores, such as cleaning, preparing food or washing up dishes. My only memory of the food is of a most wonderful salad, not a lettuce and tomato affair but a fantastic mix of greenery gathered from the fields and hedgerows.

Although I went on three expeditions, my memory is hazy of two of them but the other remains imprinted on my mind. We were on top of a high ridge and the rest of the party was sitting looking down on what is often described as a "beautiful patchwork quilt of fields and hedges". I sat alone, facing the opposite way, spellbound by a wide, open space of moorland-type scenery.

I know that on one of those walks we did 17 miles and I like to think that the other may have been longer, it certainly wasn't shorter. When our group arrived back in Chester on the Saturday evening I said brightly, "There's a dance on at Hawarden Camp tonight, shall we go?" There were no takers and after that nobody suggested that I should take more exercise.

Practically everyone smoked in those days and many men, my father included, smoked a pipe. The smell of pipe tobacco was quite attractive to some people; the same could be hardly be said of cigarette smoke even then. I was constantly being offered a cigarette and in the end I accepted one and then I was offered more and so naturally at that point I had to buy a packet myself to offer around in return. Then I was hooked! Later cigarettes became not all that plentiful and some of the cheaper brands were pretty lethal. I remember a short train journey when I was offered a cigarette by a soldier and thought I was going to pass out by the time I had finished it; it was called a Black Cat. Woodbines were an old brand of the cheaper variety that the soldiers smoked and I could cope with those. Courtesy demanded that you accepted one if offered so that you didn't appear unfriendly or superior with your own pack of Churchill No. 1 or whatever.

My brother had been smoking cigarettes since he was about ten years old, in secret of course and if he could purloin one from somewhere. He also experimented before that with some noxious substance that he crammed into a clay pipe; I don't suppose that this did his asthma much good. After a lifetime of smoking heavily, he contracted cancer of the pancreas and he said that he couldn't understand why it wasn't cancer of the lungs. I gave up the habit for good when I was 30 and was amazed to find how much more flavour my food now had. It was not all that long before research started into the effects of smoking on our health but it was a long time before the results were made public and people were scared into giving it up.

Social life was centred around the pubs and there were certainly a great many of them in Chester. People tended to have their favourite haunts and the one I and many of the people I knew frequented was patronised mainly by the Air Force. We all drank beer, spirits being in short supply and expensive. The older generation of men claimed that the beer was watered down in the war but I don't think that there was any truth in this. The atmosphere must have been pretty ghastly in a pub full of young people all smoking and drinking, but not all that heavily of course as there was a limit to what they could afford. Everyone was intent on enjoying themselves, after all nobody, particularly the airmen, knew how much longer they would live. Air crew were deemed at one time to be lucky if they survived three tours of duty.

When the pubs closed we all wended our way home or perhaps on a rare occasion went in search of something to eat. There was one place I remember that must have stayed open very late because it was known to us as The Midnight Café. It was on the rough side to say the least and it was rumoured that it might perhaps be used for immoral purposes, to put it politely.

I was expected to be home shortly after closing time if not before unless I was going to a dance at the weekend and even those didn't go on until a late hour. I have always told myself that I should be tolerant of young night-time revellers as I know there were occasions when some of us would link arms and march down the street singing, "You are my sunshine, my only sunshine". Now all those years later when I go to a Music & Movement exercise group, I find that we are often doing our stuff to that very song. So far we have been spared Vera Lynn singing "We'll meet again". I suppose the tempo is too slow. She was called the "Forces Sweetheart" and that she may well have been. Personally, I have never liked sentimental songs but I can well understand their appeal for those separated from their wives or girlfriends.

CHAPTER EIGHTEEN

It came as a bit of a bombshell when the powers that be said they were thinking of making me secretary to the new Brigadier. They then had second thoughts; that honour, if such it could be called, should go to the head of the typing pool in which case I could take over her job. I couldn't think of anything worse than being the boss of a bunch of fellow typists, most of whom would be older than I was. I was saved from either of these moves by the Brigadier himself. He wished to bring his own assistant on the grounds that it should be someone in uniform, a member of the ATS. This was how he managed to bring Diana into our ranks. Diana was the daughter of his lady friend who lived in Harley Street Mews in London.

Diana was an extremely attractive and sophisticated redhead, a couple or so years older than me. I don't know whether or not she knew that I had been in line for her job but to save any embarrassment and also because I liked her I invited her home for lunch on her first Sunday. John was home on leave that weekend and was somewhat smitten, but Diana was unobtainable and he wasn't in need of another girlfriend anyway.

I continued working for the same vehicle section but was now given an office in a small room near the front door of Fern House, from which I could be seen by people walking past to get to Oak House. It wasn't long before I shared it with a rather strange ATS girl who was supposed to assist me as I was getting rather an overload of work. The Chief Clerk arranged this and asked me to keep an eye on her which I did to the best of my ability. Apart from being strange she must have blotted her copybook in the ATS because he asked me to leave my office one day whilst he had a word with her; the upshot of this was that she made a quick exit, possibly she was discharged on health grounds or for some serious misdemeanour.

It was whilst working in this office that I experienced a bit of eyestrain and needed to wear glasses for work. This did not cost me anything because being a low-paid worker I was what was called a "panel patient". We all contributed a penny or so in the pound – I know it was a negligible sum – to something like a hospital fund and this entitled you to see a designated Panel Doctor, go to hospital or whatever was required free of charge. The National Health Service did not start until 1948 and all but the low paid were liable for their own doctors' bills, etc. I don't remember the ins and outs of the scheme but I know that I never paid for treatment, not that I recall ever being ill.

So there I was, sitting at my desk in front of the window, wearing my glasses, when one of the men who fancied himself as a bit of a ladies' man walked by, caught sight of me, turned back and came into my office. I took off my glasses and said, "No, I'm not a new bit of talent, it's still just me." Dorothy Parker's well-known saying, "Men never make passes at girls who wear glasses" is not always true.

It is difficult to remember exactly what was taking place where and when but it must have been late 1942 when I was moved yet again. I was now in a large, bright upstairs room with the rest of the section. It must have been a fairly large room because there were seven of us working there and I remember every one of my workmates vividly. Corporal Johnny Proctor was in charge and responsible for the smooth running of the department under our boss Major Vic Butler. Major Butler was a lovely, kind, middle-aged man and a chain smoker. I remember him, cigarette in mouth brushing the ash from the front of his uniform. The rest of the workforce was made up of two civilian clerks, Dot Brown and Maisie Venables, and a super ATS girl whose name I have forgotten. She had been the victim of an attempted sexual assault some time previously but had now recovered from the ordeal. It hadn't changed her sunny disposition or quenched her sense of humour. Tom was a slightly older private who was brilliant at drawing caricatures of us all, and another typist, Betty Wilson, who became a close friend.

Major Butler did not do much dictating, preferring to draft his missives in handwriting that was more or less illegible as it consisted mainly of a series of up and down strokes of his pen. So much so that one day I had made what I had thought of as some sense of the first two lines and then got completely stuck until I realised that I had been reading it upside down.

If there was a brief lull in our workload as sometimes happens in the busiest of offices Dot and Maisie would start up a rhythm with pencils and rulers, tapping table tops, ink wells, in and out trays, etc., often accompanied by the clatter of our two typewriters.

Johnny now had a girlfriend who reputedly lived in the Western Isles of Scotland and if he had a long weekend pass he would cycle all the way up there to see her. He once lent me his bike so that I could nip into the town in my lunch hour but I didn't get further than the end of the road. Apart from being larger than my bike and having a cross bar to negotiate when mounting it was a drop handle affair of the type we used to call a "here's my head, my bottom's coming" bicycle.

After a while Major Butler had a captain wished upon him as an assistant. We none of us thought that he was very bright or of much use although he was a pleasant enough man. He never seemed to read through anything we typed for him and it was agreed by all of us that he would sign his own death warrant if it was put before him. We debated on whether or not we should put this to the test but in the end we chickened out.

Betty's desk was beside the window which we usually opened, weather permitting. What distracted Betty and took her attention off the document she was copying I don't know but when she turned back to her desk it was to see it sailing out of the window, caught by a sudden gust of wind. We rushed over and watched it land at the feet of the Brigadier who was walking along the road. Our concern was that it had "SECRET" written on it in large letters. The Brigadier must have seen it land but like our Captain he did not always read what was put before him. Danger over, we were able to retrieve it with no harm done.

My one and only flutter on the horses was whilst I was in this office. A fellow from one of the other sections was acting as a bookie. I refused to join in at first and then he tried talking me into betting a shilling on a treble. I looked at him blankly and he explained that fourpence would be put on my first race and if my horse won the winnings would go on the second race and if that horse also won the total would be staked on a third horse. "Oh, all right, just this once," I said and handed over my shilling. He later came back and handed me my winnings of 30 shillings. I had struck lucky. I never gambled again. I figured it was best to quit whilst I was on top. Thirty shillings was £1.50 in today's money and it constituted a whole week's wages for me.

As Mother was in need of a break and I was beginning to feel a bit under the weather, the two of us went away for a weekend together on my winnings. We stayed in a small country pub about six miles inland from Rhyl in North Wales and did a lot of walking in the countryside. I remember the pub as being rather dark but quite comfortable and later on the Saturday evening we ventured down into the bar for a drink before closing time. The landlord called out "last orders" and when the local policeman put his head round the door he called, "time". We expected that to be the end of the evening but, no, the nice policeman came in through the back door and we all had another drink.

Dot had been a volunteer with the Auxiliary Fire Service for some time when Beb and I decided to join their ranks. We would be required to be on duty every sixth night and we could choose between admin duties and be typists or we could man the telephones and deal with the despatching of fire fighting men and vehicles if there was a fire. Beb chose Admin and I chose to join Dot on the despatch side. Having been accepted as new recruits we now had to go on a training course with other volunteers.

The course took place somewhere in the countryside and we were billeted in Nissen huts. Everyone will be familiar with those today, having seen them in many films about one war or another, but they were new to me. Ours was a bit on the chilly side but there was a stove in the middle to warm us up and of course there were the usual bunk beds. We were initiated into the procedures and jargon of the Fire Service and for some obscure reasons we had to do a spot of marching and drilling and this I quite enjoyed. The course took place over two weekends and on completion we had to be kitted out with uniforms.

They never did manage to find a hat for me so when I went on duty I would wait outside whilst Dot went in, saluting smartly and saying, "Firewoman Brown reporting for duty." She would then go to the window and chuck out her hat for me to wear, and I would go in, salute smartly and say, "Firewoman Cook reporting for duty" and that would be the end of formalities.

Learning the jargon was all very well but sometimes we would find that it had changed from one week to the next and that "glow showing" had now been replaced by "glimmer" or vice versa to indicate the severity of the fire. I was always scared stiff that I would find myself alone on duty when there was a fire and that I would make a complete bosh of it. Thank goodness that Dot was more capable and confident and that I was never put in that position. The firemen were very considerate and around two am if all seemed quiet they would stand us down and send us off to our bunks. The Fire Station at the time I joined was still in a very old building. We had a small room with a wash basin, the primitive lavatory was in a hut down the end of the yard and you staggered down there in the dark with a small torch and thanked your lucky stars that you were not the sort to be terrified by the myriads of black beetles that infested the place.

Dot was delighted that I had now replaced her previous partner. It wasn't that she disliked the girl, it was simply because she worked in a fish and chip shop and as she occupied the lower bunk bed Dot was breathing in the fumes of fish, fat and vinegar, which rather upset her. At 6 o'clock in the morning we went off duty, mounted our bikes and pedalled off home to have a bath and a bite to eat before going back to our day job. Some time later we moved to our new Headquarters where there were 'all mod cons'.

It must have been when I was away on leave or something that Dot spent an unnerving night at the Fire Station. It had been arranged that there would be an Exercise, which meant that all procedures would be carried out on paper or phone but not acted upon. Dot, as usual, did everything methodically, then was stunned to hear down the phone desperate cries of "Where the blankety blank are the fire engines, reinforcements or whatever". The Exercise had been cancelled and nobody had thought to inform Dot of the fact. Obviously, she was exonerated from all blame, but it must have been horrifying for all of them.

CHAPTER NINETEEN

To my surprise one day I received notice to appear for an interview regarding my call-up for war work, despite the fact of my being in a reserved occupation. I found myself facing two WVS women and from then on I always visualised that organisation as being staffed by either short, buxom women with large bosoms or tall, rangy ones with flat chests, so I think that must have been what those two looked like. In those long ago days nobody called anyone by their Christian names unless they knew them as friends or equals and I was a trifle surprised to hear one of these formidable women say in a rather plummy, patronising voice, "Well now Margaret I am sure that you would like to do something to help your country."

I was feeling a bit under the weather and her tone of voice irritated me somewhat, added to which

"Margaret" was not a name I responded to. I had never been called Margaret, except by my headmistress and one or two other teachers. All my life I had been called "Meg" or "Cookie" or by the formal "Miss Cook". "Of course," I replied in sugary sweet tones, "but I'm afraid that I don't have much spare time."

I then explained that I worked from nine to six for five days a week and on one evening when I would be on late duty, every Saturday morning and on every alternate Saturday afternoon and also on one Sunday morning in three. The women looked surprised and then I gave them the final blow; I did all night duty with the AFS every sixth night. They looked at each other, then one of them said, "Yes, you do seem to be doing rather a lot." She paused for thought, then added, "Perhaps you might like to join the Rangers." I looked at her blankly and she said, "The Rangers are senior Girl Guides, dear." I thanked her politely and declined.

Walking home in the blackout presented no problems; darkness was a normal part of our lives. If there was fog as well, that was a different matter. One evening when the fog was bad and the buses had to stop running, I was making my way out of the city, keeping close to the inner edge of the pavement, when I became aware of a little old lady weaving around almost in circles. I asked her where she was heading and she gave me an address that was on my way home. It was a turning off the road I would be walking up when I left the main road so I suggested that we should walk along together. She agreed gladly. The only trouble was that the old dear kept breaking free and trying to wander off into the road where she would be quite lost in the fog.

We finally made it to the beginning of her street and she told me the number of her house. Now and again there would be a slight clearance and I could count the vague outlines of the houses as we passed. No light could be shown from any building and Air Raid Wardens were always on patrol to make sure that no-one breached the rules. Black material was bought to make additional curtains to prevent any light showing to indicate to the German bombers that there was a town or help them to identify where they were. So it was understandable that doors should be closed hurriedly, but normally the occupants would extinguish the lights prior to opening the door. Finally we arrived and hoping we had settled on the right one I knocked on the door. It was opened and without a word of greeting she was let in and the door was almost slammed in my face. I groped my way back, and as I got further up the hill the fog became a little less dense and I got to thinking about the poor old lady with nobody seeming to have been worried about her being out alone on such a night or at all relieved to see her back.

That thought reminded of the saying, "There's nowt so queer as folk" and I thought of someone else who came into that category. I had once or twice met the mother of a girl with whom I was friendly; she was a nice little woman but gave me the impression that she was down-trodden and not all that self-confident. This did not altogether surprise me when I learnt that her husband grew vegetables on his allotment and insisted that she bought all that they ate from him and paid for them out of her housekeeping money.

Later on in the war we had a man called Mac living with us who came into the 'strange' category. Mother's old friend Dorothy from her Bournemouth days wrote to say that she had split up with her long-term partner and had now married someone else and, as they were in need of a place to live within travelling distance to where her husband would be working could they come to us? As I have indicated previously, accommodation was in short supply and anyone with a spare room was likely to have a stranger or two billeted on them. Mother and Father agreed that they could join us and have John's bedroom which was now available as he was in Canada.

Mac turned out to be a very large, overweight, self-satisfied man who was not above eating more than his fair share of the rationed food, whereas Dorothy was if anything even smaller than Mother. We none of us liked Mac but out of loyalty to an old friend we tolerated him and as Father was incapacitated by now their financial contribution came in handy. Unfortunately, Mac was a dishonest character who ended up in prison. I was stunned to read a paragraph in the newspaper – the Telegraph, I think – that he had forged my father's signature to make some deal, the details of which I have no recollection. He was convicted of fraud and sent to prison.

Dorothy, who was unaccountably obsessed with the man, left us to take a job as a housekeeper in order to be near the prison and visit him. She was highly amused when her wealthy employer told her that the position was hers but that she would not tolerate her having any 'followers'. This evidently was an old term to denote a male friend who might wish to court her.

CHAPTER TWENTY

Mother was not a woman to raise her voice or speak harshly to anyone; her look of disapproval was enough to lay guilt firmly at your door. It was agreed in the family that if put to it she could fell an ox at 300 paces with one of her 'looks'. She was petite and beautiful and her upbringing had led her to believe that she was delicate and this was something we accepted and therefore felt that it was not the done thing to upset Mother. There is no control quite so effective as that exercised by the vulnerable, particularly if they are kind and loving.

From an early age, I took my beliefs, likes and dislikes from my mother, not that she ever told me in so many words what I should feel about anything; it was more what was implied rather than said. Whether or not this affected my school work I am not sure but looking back I think it did. I knew she didn't like history, she much preferred geography, therefore I tried to be good at it, too, but apart from tracing maps in the early days, I was pretty hopeless. I could never remember where anything was. I might be able to know roughly where a continent was but as for knowing where exactly the countries were within it and what they were called, that was a matter of luck if I got it right. I must have been born lucky because I always managed to come near the top of the class when we had end of term exams, the other subjects having pulled my average up.

English, German and French were the subjects of Mother's choice and I could manage these without too much effort and I wasn't too bad at maths considering that she didn't care for it. In a similar way, she passed on to me her fear of cows and swimming. Interestingly, she neither listened to nor played anything by Bach as she condemned his music as being too mathematical.

I am sure that Mother never intended to influence my thinking on so many subjects but she did exactly that for many years of my childhood. Later my growing independence of mind came to a head when I asked Father one evening when we were on our own if he liked Negro spirituals. I knew that Mother didn't. "Yes, mostly I do," he answered. "A lot depends on who is singing them, of course." I found this particularly liberating, particularly as I soon discovered that we also shared a liking for Bach. Because I loved Mother and was sure that she loved me, I still spent the rest of my life not hurting or upsetting her and to this day I can be momentarily hesitant to express an opinion when I do not yet know the questioner's views on the subject.

On the evenings that I wasn't out with my friends I would either read or listen to the wireless with my parents. We listened to a wide variety of music and I particularly remember being enthralled by some of the operas that were broadcast. I was familiar with some of the music from several, such as La traviata, Carmen and The Tales of Hoffman but The Flying Dutchman was new to me and I sat listening to that for the first time one evening with Father and was enthralled. We didn't share the same taste in books as we did in music; he never did convert me to Dickens.

Father was not a big man but his strength to weight ratio was very high so when one day he came in from the garden and on trying with difficulty to open the dining room door said, "What's the matter with this damned door handle?" we realised that something was wrong. It was the start of his osteoarthritis. It came upon him remarkably quickly after he had broken a rib whilst sawing a branch off one of the pear trees. The doctor said that the breaking of a bone was quite often the cause of the onset of osteoarthritis. Whether this was a theory at that time or a fact I don't know. It spread incredibly quickly and before long he developed rheumatoid arthritis as well, so he became both incapacitated and in pain which got progressively worse as the years went by.

The doctors used Father as a guinea-pig, trying out different treatments on him in the interests of science and of course to help him but sometimes with disastrous effects. Gold injections which they hoped would be a wonder cure resulted in toxic poisoning. They then decided that this was connected with the teeth; somebody in the past had benefited from having all of theirs extracted but it didn't help Father. He then had an abscess on the lung and was in a ghastly hospital in Liverpool. They cured his abscess but the treatment that they gave him made his arthritis worse. He was amazing throughout all this time. There was no self-pity, just annoyance and a fighting spirit. Mother was equally amazing. She cared for him without complaint for years, until he died aged 56.

Unlike Mother, my father would tell me if I was doing something wrong and explain why. He would speak firmly and quietly and call me 'Margaret' instead of 'Meg'. I knew better than to offend in that particular way again. You could talk with him about all sorts of things and sometimes we sat up a bit too late at night, putting the world to rights. I recall one evening Mother getting up from her armchair and saying, "If you two are going to go on arguing, I'm going to bed." Father told her gently, "We are not arguing, we are discussing." Actually, we did sometimes take opposing sides on a subject as a way of putting different views across.

On one such evening I remember quite clearly Mother getting up from her chair without a word but giving us one of her looks. "Oh dear," Father said in a low voice as she left the room. "I can feel a North wind blowing." She must have heard him but she said nothing; perhaps he got a repeat look later when he joined her upstairs.

I don't think Mother ever completely understood Father. She told me years after he died that he was a tough character, without a nerve in his body and not at all sentimental or sensitive. My view of him was slightly different. For example, I was with him in the shed-cum-garage in Chester when he was sorting things out. It was then that he showed me the old family Bible, something which he must have kept hidden away all those years since his parents died. I picked up a box, asking what was in it. "Oh," he said, "those are my oil paints." I didn't know he had ever painted and they must have been all dried up by then, but they were something else which he had hung on to for old times' sake.

I don't know whether Mother altogether understood me either, perhaps she may have known my brother better as she had spent so much time with him when he was in Bournemouth with her as a child and when he had to be home from school with his asthma. But there was one advantage I had over John. Whilst she was always extremely possessive of him she didn't become possessive of me until she was about sixty and John was far away in Canada.

CHAPTER TWENTY-ONE

It was probably in late 1942 or early 1943 that Betty Wilson met her future husband, Ted Wright. He was stationed in Wrexham, to the south of Chester, on the borders of Wales, where he was undergoing the last stages of training to become an Army officer. Ted was about 6'2", tall enough to be nicknamed 'Tiny' Wright by his fellow would-be officers, although he would not be considered particularly tall by today's standards as in the intervening years both men and women have become taller and their feet and hands correspondingly larger. On several occasions Ted waited for Betty outside our office and he must have had a superior manner or given off unfriendly vibes because not one of our Army staff liked the look of him. Indeed one of our warrant officers referred to him as 'that supercilious bastard'. Ted duly got his commission and was posted elsewhere. Betty and I had become friends and spent many evenings in each other's company so of course I met Ted and I must confess that I didn't like him either.

In 1943 the Battle of the Atlantic was in full swing with the advantage first with one side and then the other. Much of our shipping was lost but we were successfully sinking the German U boats and as much as anything it was a case of which of us could build new vessels to replace the sunken ones more quickly. Our factories and ship-building yards were working flat out and we were winning the race. The American Air Force was destroying the Japanese air power and they were forced into fighting in the jungles and mountains. The Soviets had won the battle of Stalingrad and had started their drive to expel the Germans from Russian soil. We had won in North Africa and were thus able to invade Sicily from there. Mussolini was forced to resign and we signed an Armistice with Italy. We then made a landing on the mainland but met with such resistance from the Germans that we suffered very heavy losses and it wasn't until 1944 that we could break through and reach Rome and fight our way northwards. However, we all felt far more optimistic about the eventual outcome of the war and it was in this happier time that Betty married Ted.

Ted's family had visited Chester when he and Betty became engaged and that was when we first met. I saw them again at the wedding. Ted's younger brother, Peter, was his best man and not yet in the forces. He was working for a large firm of building contractors and this was considered to be a 'reserved occupation', which meant that you were not liable for call up to the armed services.

Peter was tall, slim and fair-haired and not the least like his brother in either appearance or manner. We were attracted to each other to the extent that I was invited to spend a long weekend with him and his parents in their bungalow in Hertfordshire. They were Londoners and had decided to evacuate to a safer place, which must have been in the countryside as I remember that they had oil lamps for lighting, but apart from that their home had all 'mod cons', to use estate agent jargon.

Mr Wright commuted to work in North London each day. He also worked in the building trade and was the Company Secretary of a fairly large construction firm. It was an enjoyable weekend. I liked Peter's parents, who were about ten years older than mine, and they apparently approved of me. Peter visited us in Chester, seemingly gaining the approval of my parents; at any rate, they didn't say anything against him and, as I have indicated, Mother was in no way possessive of me in those days so she didn't scare him off in the way she used to dispose of John's girlfriends. I cannot recall the reason why Peter and I split up. I only know that something didn't seem right and I dropped him.

Time passed and it was now well into 1944 and on June 6th, D-Day, British and American troops invaded Normandy and US and Canadian troops landed in the south of France, attacking from the Mediterranean. However, all was not going so well in Britain. The Germans had developed their secret weapon, the V.1, an unguided flying bomb which they launched against London from June 1944 onwards. This was followed by the V.2, which had a pre-guidance system and thousands of civilians were killed by these missiles between then and March 1945.

By now I had forgotten all about Peter until one evening when I was cycling homeward in the pouring rain with Bev. We were held up at the traffic lights and she asked me what I would do at the end of the war. To my complete astonishment, I heard myself reply, "I shall marry Peter Wright." She said that she thought that I no longer liked him and that we had split up long ago. I agreed that this was true but that he would turn up again. When I said all this I had no wish to ever meet him again let alone marry him, it had just come into my mind unbidden as an inevitable fact. I then dismissed it all as a stupid thing to have said.

Some months later I received a letter from Peter full of apologies, telling me that he was now in the Air Force and asking if we could meet up if he came to Chester. We did meet again and became engaged later in the year. I insisted that we would wait until the following summer before marrying as I considered that we were both young and needed to spend more time together before making such a commitment.

Unlike Ted, Peter never became an officer; he was what was known as an A.C. Plonk, meaning that he was an Aircraftsman 2, the lowest of the low, and he worked as a radar mechanic. When I took a photograph of him to show to my workmates, telling them that he was Ted's brother, I wondered whether they would be prejudiced against him. I needn't have worried, everybody, including those in the Army, reckoned that he was totally different by the look of him and they gave me their blessing.

My unexpected certainty that I would marry Peter was not the first time nor would it be the last when I knew in advance what would happen or, even more strangely, was suddenly aware of something that was actually happening somewhere else.   The first occasion was when I was about nine years old and walking in the fields with my parents near our house at Brookside.   Roger, our Airedale Terrier, suddenly bounded off and we could see him trying to get into a hole in the ground.   It was such a tight squeeze that we were all afraid that he would get stuck and would be unable to wriggle himself back out again.   I was horrified and turned my back, unable to watch. Whether I prayed or merely wished for good to happen, as I always did when it was my turn to pull a wishbone, I do not know.   What I do know is that suddenly I knew that all would be well and that when I turned back Roger would emerge head first.   I turned around and sure enough Roger did come out head first and I was the only one not at all surprised.

Another example was a long distance one during the war when John was in Canada.   I was just getting into bed and as I started to lie down I felt any icy shock and sat bolt upright again.   At that moment I had known that something had happened to John and that he was hurt.   It was an awful feeling but it didn't last long.   A feeling of peace came over me and I knew that he would be all right, that he would recover.   We didn't hear from my brother for some time and both Mother and Father were beginning to worry.   I didn't say anything for fear of being thought stupid but I knew that he had been unable to write because of what had happened to him and that he would write as soon as he was able. When we finally received his airmail letter, he told us that that he had been crossing the airfield when something penetrated his eye and he had lost most of the sight in it which was why he hadn't been able to write before.

There have been other times in my life when I had known something in advance or at the time of it happening, two of which were devastating, none of the other occasions were particularly dramatic, just strange. I have not had any such experiences for a great many years which is something of a relief – sufficient unto the day, etc. I certainly do not want to know of any impending doom and if there is something good on the horizon it can just be a happy surprise.

CHAPTER TWENTY-TWO

The war in Europe ended in May 1945 and on June 8th Peter and I were married in the church at Upton. We spent a week honeymooning in Weston-Super-Mare, not because we wished to go to that Somerset seaside town more than anywhere else but because everybody was now free to move around and hotel accommodation was in such short supply that you went wherever rooms were available. Strangely, I cannot recall that week, but the result of it was that I had immediately become pregnant.

At the beginning of July, I secured my release from working for the Ministry of Defence. I had discovered the little known fact that now that the war in Europe was over, civilians could leave their job if they were married. Previously, the only way out was using what was called "discharge under paragraph eleven", which signified to all and sundry that you were pregnant. Not wishing to endure the ribald comments of the whole Branch over my very rapid pregnancy, I let it be known to Personnel that I was aware of this new freedom and was permitted to leave without having to tell anybody that I was pregnant.

Peter was stationed at an airfield near Earls Colne in Essex and found lodgings for us in the village of Great Tey with the local cobbler and his wife. The evening that I arrived she told me that she had to go into hospital the following day and therefore I would be responsible for cooking the meals for her husband as well as for us. This terrified me as I thought that I would have to use her ancient oil-burning contraption, but my sanity was saved when she relented and decided that I could use her equally ancient electric cooker. The hospital appointment was in connection with the possibility of an operation to help her conceive the child she desperately wanted before she was too old. When she discovered that I was pregnant, it didn't exactly endear me to her heart.

Her husband was a strange-looking man who rarely spoke, in fact he seemed to us to be a trifle weird. He bore a strong resemblance to the mad brother in the play "Arsenic and Old Lace", which was currently showing in London. Unfortunately, he told his wife that I had cooked the best meal that he had eaten for a long time; this was a bit tactless, if not downright idiotic of the man, but I don't think that he was very bright at the best of times. The diet which she provided for us consisted almost entirely of tinned pilchards with cucumbers and tomatoes from the garden. It was here that I had my second encounter with an outside loo. There must have been an indoor washbasin as I don't remember having to wash in the kitchen sink, that was a treat yet to come.

In August the war with Japan ended and Peter and I walked to the village of Little Tey and downed a glass of beer to celebrate. Great Tey had neither a pub nor a church; these were to be found in Little Tey which must have been the larger and more important village in spite of its name. We were careful to ensure that our landlady did not realise that we had been to the pub as she and her husband were strict teetotallers and we feared that they might throw us out if they knew that we had been drinking.

Shortly after this, Peter found us somewhere to live in Earls Colne. We shared a dilapidated old terrace cottage with another airman and his wife until he was posted elsewhere. We then had the place to ourselves apart from now sharing it with the colonies of mice that could be heard scampering behind the walls. Unfortunately, they didn't spend all their time behind the walls; they were quick to put in an appearance if there was any food about. When carrying food from the pantry under the stairs to the kitchen, you had to take a wire mesh cover with you to place over it while you went back for a second load; if you didn't, the mice would come out before you returned and start nibbling away at the food. This may sound like an exaggeration but it's perfectly true. I went into the kitchen one evening with my torch, there being no electric light in there, and after making sure there was sufficient money in the gas meter I bent down, opened the oven door and came face-to-face with the mouse that was sitting inside. I left hurriedly and went back to the sitting-room.

The sitting-room was not always 'sittable' in. There was something radically wrong with the chimney as it had to be swept every two weeks or so otherwise you would be asphyxiated by the smoke. Coal and coke were in short supply so we couldn't always light a fire, not a large one anyway. We once ran out of fuel completely but Peter solved the problem by nicking some from the Base. He tied up the bottom of his trousers and cycled home with some lumps of coal down each trouser leg. It was fortunate that it was a dark night as he had to travel home bare-legged with his trousers slung around his neck.

The kitchen was a built-in extension with a piece of sacking over the hole in the roof. The sink was about two inches deep with only a cold tap. Water had to be boiled on the stove for washing the dishes or oneself. It was no wonder that we lived as frugally as possible so that we could afford to take the train to London now and again to stay with Peter's parents and luxuriate in a bath. Our loo was a six-foot drop in a shed at the end of the back yard and it was no joke being pregnant and making the journey during the night, pregnancy having brought on more of a need to use it. One good thing about it was that unlike the old one at the Fire Station in Chester there were no black beetles in residence. It wasn't too bad in the summer but later on when it was cold and we had a fall of snow it wasn't an enjoyable experience.

Our predecessors in the cottage were not bothered by the lack of an indoor toilet or bathroom. They told us that they had been accustomed to such conditions. They came from a Midland or Northern town where, before the war, many of the houses for workers were built in rows with a back alley between them and the lavatories therein were often shared with other families. Early in the century, when electricity first became available in houses, most of the populace still had oil or gas lamps and having an indoor bathroom or toilet would not have been thought of as a normal way of life. It was more likely that there would be an oval-shaped tub stored in the kitchen which would be filled with hot water so that the family could have a bath, otherwise they had to make do with washing at the kitchen sink. We had one of those zinc tubs in our cottage but it had a hole in it.

Peter neither then nor subsequently was a man to make friends or socialise and there was only one other airman that I met. Jack Barbero was probably of Spanish descent and he had been to Spain to fight in the 1936-39 civil war. I don't know which side he was on because I don't remember him discussing it with us, which was rather a pity. Sometimes I would get up early in the morning, go down to the kitchen and find that Jack had let himself in and was washing a pair of socks or underpants in the kitchen sink. He would turn up some evenings with a pile of mushrooms that he had gathered and a tin of dried egg that he had filched from the RAF kitchen and we would eat a delicious meal of fried mushrooms and scrambled eggs on toast. Tins of dried egg powder came from America and were much appreciated by us all, as apart from making scrambled egg you could use the powder to make a cake now and again.

Mother and Father came to visit us one weekend and Mother's comments were pretty scathing. "Oh!" she said, "I wouldn't live here for the brightest man on earth", adding, "and Peter certainly isn't that!" Thanks, Mum! They stayed at The Cups Hotel in Colchester and we were having a drink with them in the lounge when Noel Coward (the famous playwright, actor and composer) made an entrance with two or three friends. He stood, gazed around – one felt that he wanted to make sure that he was noticed – and then looked directly at us. Mother thought that he was directing his gaze at her but knowing something of the man's reputation, I thought that he might well be looking at Peter. I didn't disillusion Mother, but I was pretty sure that I was right.

CHAPTER TWENTY-THREE

My brother remained in Canada until the war ended. He was stationed in Winnipeg where he met and fell in love with Sara Louise. He wrote to Mother and Father telling them that he had become engaged and in a separate airmail letter to me he said, "Don't worry, Mother will accept her; she will know that there is no alternative, that it is a fait accompli." He sent them a photograph of Sara Louise and she looked lovely, kind and intelligent; when we met her we found that she possessed all of these attributes. When the war in Europe ended, she came to England on the first passenger boat to cross the Atlantic and lived with Mother and Father until John was demobilised and they could marry and be together.

In August I went back to Chester for a long weekend and met Sara Louise. I must confess that for the first and only time in my life I experienced a tinge of jealousy. It was obvious that my parents had taken a great liking to her and whilst I was accustomed to feeling that John was special to Mother I now realised that I had felt that perhaps I was special to Father and I was afraid that Sara Louse had usurped that position. I didn't blame her or them but it knocked my self-esteem, which had never been very high, a little further down. I soon got over it, realising that I was being silly and that no comparisons were being made. I was still the daughter they loved and she was the daughter-in-law they loved.

That weekend I told Mother that I was pregnant. She was not best pleased. I remember her words, which I am sure that she later regretted. "I thought that you would have had more sense. Don't bring it home for me to look after." I was heartbroken at this rejection and sat on my bed and sobbed. Even on the train returning to Essex I had difficulty keeping the tears at bay. I am sure it was only shocked surprise that caused her to say what she did but I vowed that I would never ask her for help. Actually I didn't need to, she was a wonderful grandmother and adored both my children.

In December our landlord wanted repossession of the cottage in Earls Colne and Peter had to live on the RAF base again. Mum and Dad, as I called his parents, invited me to live with them in Southgate and made me feel very welcome. I grew very fond of them both.

Mum was a chain smoker and could keep a cigarette in her mouth with no difficulty no matter what task she was performing and the smoke never seemed to get in her eyes. She had a sister, Auntie Tott, who worked in one of the big London stores and lived in Acton with her husband who was a hairdresser. Mum used to go all the way over there to have her hair cut and coloured. She didn't make the journey very often and had quite a wide strip of grey along her parting which didn't worry her at all and it somehow seemed to suit her.

Like my mother, Mum was an excellent cook. Her roast potatoes were particularly delicious and no matter how you tried to copy everything she did you could never achieve the same perfection. However, she reckoned my Yorkshire puddings were better that hers so I got the job of making those for lunch every Sunday. Unlike Mother she was a completely unimaginative cook so our corned beef ration was used to make sandwiches for supper every Sunday evening.

Because I was pregnant I had a special ration book entitling me to an extra amount of some foods as our government wanted the next generation to be strong and healthy. I cannot remember whether this continued after the baby was born or whether the child had a separate ration book.

About midnight on the 6th of March I lay in bed experiencing the start of labour pains, but having been told that these would probably go on for many hours I waited until I heard Dad moving about around 6.30 in the morning and then I called out to him. He felt he should do something helpful and as it was bitterly cold he decided to light the fire in my bedroom and bring me a cup of tea. The fire had not been used for many years and almost exploded so he had to give up on that idea. By nine o'clock I was hopping from foot to foot and Dad decided to call an ambulance as there was so much snow and ice on the ground and he didn't fancy driving the car. I don't suppose it would have started anyway as I don't think he had driven it since the beginning of the war.

Because the war had ended in May 1945 and many of our troops were back in Britain there was a bumper crop of babies in March and all the hospital maternity wards were full so I had to go to a nursing home owned by the doctor. This was fine apart from the fact that they had run out of fuel and there was no heating whatsoever in the building.

I continued to live with Mum and Dad until my son John was about three months old, by which time Peter's brother Ted had come home. It now seemed a good idea to return to Chester to live with Mother and Father until Peter was demobilised and we could be together again.

When the war ended there was a great shortage of housing, particularly in those areas that had suffered devastating bombing raids and building and construction companies could apply for former employees to be demobilised early so that reconstruction could get under way. Peter's old firm applied for his release and sent him to Plymouth to work as a quantity surveyor. We rented a couple of rooms, with the use of the kitchen and bathroom in a bungalow in the village of Plymstock. About six months later, Peter joined his father's old firm, Rowley Brothers, in the borough of Wood Green in North London. The company had built and still owned a street of small terrace houses near their offices and we were able to rent one of them.

The winter of 1946/47 was bitterly cold. Electricity was only available for a limited number of hours a day and coke and coal were still in short supply. Many of us had portable Valor oil stoves, which we could use when all else failed. We queued up for the oil when word passed around that there had been a delivery at the local hardware store. Bread was rationed for the first time where we lived and there was also a temporary potato shortage; fortunately not at the same time as the bread rationing. Many people believed that our butter ration was being reduced because we were sending food to Germany. We probably were because we learned later that in some areas the German people had been in danger of starving. Meat was rationed but offal wasn't and neither was fish which was mainly frozen cod imported from Iceland. We never went hungry and it was a healthy diet. Children and expectant mothers had free cod liver oil and bottles of concentrated orange juice.

In 1948 we bought a house in the London suburb of Southgate with a mortgage from Rowley Brothers. At that time empty property was liable to be requisitioned by the council or the Government and sometimes squatters moved in and couldn't be evicted. As a result, an incoming family's removal van parked up behind the outgoing one to make sure that there was no opportunity for squatters to move in. The house was extremely dirty and the first few hours were spent cleaning up a bedroom for John to sleep in and making the kitchen reasonably hygienic. The pantry had what I thought was very dark, almost black, linoleum on the shelves but when I scrubbed them I found that it was light green underneath the dirt. There was a thick, felt-like layer of dust on the small side window-sill in our bedroom where presumably some furniture had stood. The previous owners were a solicitor and his elegant, well-dressed wife, who, we were told later, spent all her time playing golf and socialising. She certainly spent none of it cleaning the house.

Our daughter, Margaret, was born in July 1949 and we continued to live in Southgate until both Peter and his brother had a serious disagreement with the Rowley Brothers and left the company. This was a worrying time and we were down to our last twenty pounds when Peter's and Ted's claims for the money owed to them were settled out of court. We moved away from London and bought a house in Godalming in Surrey, from where Peter commuted to London by car each day.

Father's health was steadily deteriorating, as well as having decreasing mobility due to both his rheumatoid and his osteoarthritis he had suffered from an enlarged spleen and an abscess on his lungs. When we moved to Godalming our house was large enough to accommodate my parents as well as us and Peter with his usual kindness and generosity suggested that they should live with us. The children were delighted.

Eventually Father's doctors considered that he should be living in a drier area than Surrey so my parents moved into hotels in different places to see whether Father would be in less pain somewhere else. They finally settled in Bexhill on the south coast and at first the climate seemed to suit Father better. It wasn't very long though before his health got worse, his weight dropped to under seven stone and he was in unbearable pain. He finally passed away in 1953. Both John and Margaret had loved him dearly and though relieved and thankful that he wasn't suffering any more they felt the loss quite deeply.

Mother's friends Ida and Jack Tustin had bought a large house in Bournemouth which they had converted into flatlets. These consisted mainly of a very large bed-sitting room, a small kitchen and a bathroom. So Mother went back to Bournemouth and made her new home in one of them. It was a beautiful flat, opening onto the garden and large enough for her to take her beloved piano out of storage and be able to play again.

In late 1953 Peter joined a different company and was appointed managing director of their new Canadian branch in Edmonton, Alberta. In January 1954 we set sail in the old Empress of Britain. A completely new style of living was now beginning for us and the children and for our Boxer dog who of course emigrated, too.

MEG MANLY

80900818R00100

Made in the USA
Columbia, SC
24 November 2017